Low Budget Startups

C.J. SPENCER

INDEX

Introduction 1

Blogging: From Passion to Profit.................................... 4

Creating and Selling Online Courses: Share
Your Expertise with the World 8

E-Commerce and Dropshipping: Retail for the Digital Age .13

YouTube: Building a Brand through Video 18

Podcasting: Growing Your Audience through Voice 23

Affiliate Marketing: Earning through Strategic
Partnerships... 28

Freelance Writing: Turning Words into Income 33

Graphic Design: Monetizing Creativity Online 37

Virtual Assistant Services: Providing Remote
Business Support 41

Transcription Services: Turning Audio into Text................46

Voiceover Services: Profiting from Your Voice 51

Coaching and Consulting: Guiding Others to Success........ 55

Web Development and Design: Creating
Digital Experiences 59

Stock Photography: Selling Your Images 63

Print on Demand: Selling Custom Merchandise
without Inventory.. 67

App Development: Creating and Monetizing Digital
Solutions 71

SEO Consulting: Helping Businesses Grow Online............... 76

SaaS (Software as a Service): Creating
Subscription-Based Tools 79

Domain Flipping: Trading Digital Real Estate........................82

Self-Publishing: Becoming an Author in the Digital Age.....85

Membership Sites: Building Exclusive Communities
and Recurring Income..88

Fitness Coaching: Taking Training to the Digital World........91

Social Media Marketing: Helping Brands Grow Digitally.....94

Digital Products: Creating and Selling Online Assets.......... 97

E-Book Publishing: Profiting from Digital Books................100

Podcasting: Sharing Stories and Building an Audience ...104

Email Marketing: Building and Engaging Your Audience.. 107

Freelance Services: Turning Skills into Income...................110

The Journey to Building an Online Business 113

Glossary (Alphabetical Order)...115

INTRODUCTION

In today's fast-moving digital world, opportunities to build a successful online venture are more accessible than ever. What once required massive startup capital, complex logistics, and layers of red tape can now be accomplished with minimal financial resources, a solid idea, and a bit of grit.

This book is designed to help you overcome the most common barriers that stop aspiring entrepreneurs in their tracks. Whether it's concerns about not having enough money to invest, fears of navigating the crowded digital marketplace, or doubts about your own ability to manage a business, Zero-Cost Startups provides solutions that allow you to take action today.

The goal is simple: empower you to create an income stream that can grow over time, without spending a fortune to get started. With this guide, you'll discover 28 business models that require little to no upfront costs—strategies that have been proven by real-world entrepreneurs who, just like you, started from scratch.

We will cover everything from freelancing and digital products to e-commerce and affiliate marketing, providing you with practical steps to get started in minutes. But that's not all. This book also explores crucial topics such as how to market your new business, ways to scale as you grow, and how to avoid the common pitfalls that can derail new ventures.

Each chapter of this volume is packed with actionable insights, guiding you through the essential aspects of building an online business. Whether you're looking to supplement your income or replace your 9-to-5, the models laid out here are designed to be flexible, allowing you to start small and scale at your own pace. Best of all, these business ideas require minimal technical expertise, so you don't need to be a seasoned entrepreneur or tech guru to succeed.

Why this book? The answer is simple: most people are held back by the fear that starting a business requires a substantial financial risk. While traditional businesses often come with overhead costs, the beauty of the digital age is that the barrier to entry has dramatically decreased. You can now launch a business with little to no initial investment—just your time, effort, and a willingness to learn and adapt.

This book is for the dreamers, the go-getters, and the side-hustlers who are ready to break free from the traditional path. If you've ever felt overwhelmed by the thought of starting a business or hesitated because of the perceived costs, This manuscript will show you how to build something meaningful and profitable without overextending yourself financially.

By the time you finish this book, you'll not only have a list of ideas but also the confidence to take that first step toward building your online empire. These are not theoretical concepts—they are practical, proven methods that thousands of entrepreneurs have used to launch their own ventures. With the right mindset and a clear plan, you can transform these low-cost business models into a sustainable source of income, allowing you to achieve the freedom and flexibility you've always dreamed of.

So, whether you're a budding entrepreneur, someone looking to build a side hustle, or a seasoned professional ready for a new challenge, this book is your roadmap to success. Let's get started on turning your idea into reality, one step at a time. Welcome to the world of low-cost startups!

BLOGGING

From Passion to Profit

B logging has become a cornerstone of the digital economy, providing a platform for individuals to share their thoughts, experiences, and expertise with the world. What began as an online diary for many has evolved into a multi-million-dollar industry, with bloggers profiting from a combination of ads, affiliate marketing, sponsored posts, and digital products. But blogging isn't just about writing—it's about building a brand, cultivating a loyal audience, and positioning yourself as an authority in your niche.

The first step in starting a blog is selecting a niche that you're both passionate about and that has market demand. A successful blog needs focus. The broader your topic, the harder it will be to build a dedicated readership. Think of a niche that excites you enough to write about consistently and that people are searching for. For example, if you're passionate about fitness, narrowing down your focus to something like "yoga for beginners" or "vegan bodybuilding" can help you stand out in a crowded marketplace.

Once your niche is identified, you'll need to establish your blog's tone and style. This is where your unique voice comes into play. Readers come to blogs not just for information but for the personal touch that only you can provide. Your style could be informative and data-driven, lighthearted and humorous, or deeply personal and reflective—what matters is that it resonates with your audience.

After establishing your niche and tone, content creation becomes the main focus. Consistency is key. Blogs that grow tend to post regularly, and each post should provide real value. Whether you're solving a problem for your readers or offering entertainment, your content needs to be engaging. Readers should feel that your posts offer them something they can't easily find elsewhere.

SEO (Search Engine Optimization) is also critical for your blog's growth. Learning how to optimize your posts with the right keywords, meta tags, and headings will help your blog appear higher in search engine results, making it easier for people to discover your content. The more visibility you gain through SEO, the more organic traffic your blog will receive.

Monetization is the next big step for successful bloggers. One of the most common ways to monetize a blog is through affiliate marketing. This involves promoting products or services on your blog and earning a commission from sales generated through your unique affiliate links. The trick here is to promote products that are directly related to your niche and that your audience will find valuable. For instance, a tech blogger could promote software tools, while a fashion blogger might recommend clothing lines.

Ads are another popular revenue stream, particularly for blogs that receive a high volume of traffic. Programs like Google AdSense allow you to display ads on your blog, earning money based on impressions and clicks. However, to make a significant income from ads, you'll need a substantial readership, as earnings per click tend to be small.

Sponsored posts offer another revenue opportunity, particularly as your blog grows and gains authority in its niche. Brands may pay you to write about their products or services, giving them exposure to your audience. It's important to maintain transparency with your readers by clearly labeling sponsored content, and only promoting products you genuinely believe in to avoid losing their trust.

Another lucrative way to monetize a blog is by creating and selling digital products, such as e-books, guides, or online courses. These products allow you to package your expertise and sell it directly to your readers. For example, a food blogger might create a cookbook filled with their best recipes, or a travel blogger could sell an e-guide on how to travel the world on a budget. Selling digital products can be particularly profitable because, after the initial creation, there are little to no costs associated with distribution.

Growing your blog's audience requires more than just writing great content—it requires marketing. Social media platforms like Instagram, Facebook, Twitter, and Pinterest can be incredibly effective tools for promoting your blog posts and engaging with your audience. Use these platforms to share behind-the-scenes insights, ask questions, and interact with your readers. Building a community around your blog fosters loyalty and encourages your audience to share your content with others.

Email marketing is another powerful tool for growing and retaining an audience. By offering something of value—

such as a free e-book, guide, or exclusive content—you can encourage visitors to sign up for your mailing list. With a growing list of email subscribers, you can directly promote new blog posts, special offers, and products, keeping your audience engaged and driving traffic back to your site.

Of course, blogging isn't without its challenges. One of the biggest hurdles new bloggers face is the slow build-up of traffic. It's common for new bloggers to feel discouraged if they don't see immediate results. However, patience is key. Most successful blogs take months or even years to gain traction. Persistence, combined with continuous learning and improving your craft, will eventually pay off.

Another challenge is managing the workload. Blogging requires a lot of behind-the-scenes work, from content creation and editing to promoting posts, managing social media accounts, and responding to comments. Many bloggers find that outsourcing tasks such as website maintenance or social media management allows them to focus on what they do best: creating great content.

In conclusion, blogging can be a deeply rewarding business for those who are passionate about their niche and willing to put in the work. The key to success lies in consistency, authenticity, and continuously providing value to your audience. With the right strategy, blogging can turn from a simple hobby into a profitable career, allowing you to share your passion with the world while earning a substantial income.

CREATING AND SELLING ONLINE COURSES

Share Your Expertise with the World

The digital landscape has made knowledge one of the most valuable currencies. People are hungry to learn new skills, improve their abilities, and gain expertise in a variety of fields. As a result, creating and selling online courses has become one of the most lucrative and fulfilling business opportunities in the modern age. Whether you're an expert in a professional field, a hobbyist with unique skills, or someone with a passion for teaching, online courses allow you to share your knowledge with the world—and get paid for it.

The beauty of creating an online course is that once it's developed, it can generate revenue for you for months, or even years, with minimal additional work. However, the road to a successful course requires careful planning, an understanding of your audience, and a knack for creating engaging content that resonates with learners.

The first step in creating an online course is identifying your area of expertise. What can you teach that others are willing to pay to learn? Often, people mistakenly believe they need to be the foremost expert in a field to create a course, but in reality, all you need is a practical level of expertise that allows you to teach something of value. Think about the problems you've solved, the skills you've developed, and the knowledge you have that could be useful to others. For example, if you're a digital marketing professional, you could create a course on mastering social media ads. If you're a photographer, a course on using natural light to enhance photos could attract both beginners and seasoned photographers.

Once you've identified your topic, you'll need to research your potential audience. Understanding who your course is for will help you tailor your content to their needs and learning preferences. What challenges do they face? What gaps in knowledge do they have? If you're developing a course for beginners, you'll need to break down complex concepts into easily digestible lessons. For more advanced learners, you may want to focus on niche topics that provide deeper insights into your field.

The next step is structuring your course. This is where many would-be course creators get stuck. A well-organized course breaks down a subject into clear, logical modules that guide learners through the material. Start with the basics and gradually introduce more complex ideas, ensuring that each module builds upon the last. For example, if you're teaching graphic design, your course might begin with an overview of design principles, move on to tutorials on specific software, and then progress to advanced techniques for branding and marketing.

One of the most effective ways to create engaging content is through video. Video-based learning has proven to be more effective than text-based methods because it allows students to see concepts in action. Video also helps you build a personal connection with your learners. They get to see your face, hear your voice, and relate to you as an instructor. However, video isn't the only format you should consider. Combining video lessons with written materials, downloadable resources, and quizzes can make your course more dynamic and help reinforce learning.

To create high-quality videos, you don't need a full studio setup. Many successful course creators use nothing more than a decent camera (or even a smartphone) and a good microphone. Lighting is important, too—natural light often works well, but if you're filming indoors, invest in some affordable lighting equipment to ensure your videos are bright and professional. And remember, you don't have to be perfect. What matters most is the clarity and value of the information you're providing.

After your course is structured and your content created, the next challenge is selecting the right platform to sell it on. There are several platforms available that allow you to host and sell online courses with ease. Platforms like **Teachable**, **Udemy**, and **Skillshare** provide a ready-made structure for uploading and distributing your course, as well as tools for tracking student progress, managing payments, and offering certificates of completion. These platforms are ideal for beginners because they handle much of the technical work for you, including hosting and marketing.

Alternatively, you could choose to host your course on your own website using tools like **Thinkific** or **Kajabi**. While this option requires more technical setup, it gives you complete control over your branding, pricing, and the student experience. It's a good choice for those who already have an established audience or want more flexibility in how they present and sell their course.

Once your course is live, marketing becomes your primary focus. It's not enough to create a fantastic course—you need to attract students to enroll. Social media is a powerful tool for promoting your course, especially if you can leverage platforms like Instagram, Facebook, or LinkedIn, depending on where your audience spends their time. Content marketing, such as writing blog posts or creating free YouTube tutorials that offer a preview of your teaching style, can also help generate interest in your course.

Building an email list is another essential marketing strategy. By offering something of value—such as a free mini-course, a webinar, or an informative PDF—you can encourage potential students to join your mailing list. From there, you can nurture those leads by sending them regular content that demonstrates your expertise and encourages them to enroll in your full course.

Pricing is another crucial consideration. Many course creators struggle to find the right price point. Charge too little, and you risk undervaluing your content; charge too much, and you might scare off potential students. A good approach is to research what other courses in your niche are charging and position your course accordingly. Some creators also offer tiered pricing, with a basic version of the course at a lower price and premium options (such as one-on-one coaching or additional resources) at a higher price point.

Creating an online course is a rewarding venture that allows you to share your knowledge with others while generating passive income. But the key to success lies in planning, creating quality content, and marketing your course effectively. While the process can take time and effort, once your course is up and running, it can provide you with a steady income for years to come, and the satisfaction of knowing you've helped others learn and grow.

E-Commerce and Dropshipping

Retail for the Digital Age

E-commerce has changed the retail industry, offering entrepreneurs the chance to sell products online without needing a physical storefront. Of the various models available, dropshipping has emerged as one of the most accessible ways to get started. By allowing store owners to sell products without managing inventory or handling shipping, dropshipping provides a low-risk entry point into e-commerce. However, while it simplifies many aspects of running a business, dropshipping also comes with its own unique set of challenges that aspiring entrepreneurs must navigate to achieve success.

In a traditional retail business, owners typically purchase products in bulk, store them in a warehouse, and ship them to customers as orders come in. This model requires a significant upfront investment in inventory, as well as the logistics of storing and shipping products. Dropshipping, on the other hand, operates differently. As a dropshipper, you don't hold any inventory. Instead, when a customer makes a purchase from your online store, you place an order with a third-party supplier, who then ships the product directly to your customer. You act as the middleman, managing the online store, marketing, and customer relationships, but the supplier handles all the logistics.

The beauty of dropshipping lies in its simplicity and affordability. Without the need to invest in inventory, you can start an online store with minimal upfront costs. This makes it an attractive option for new entrepreneurs who want to test the waters before committing significant resources. However, it's important to understand that while dropshipping minimizes financial risk, it doesn't eliminate the challenges of running a successful e-commerce business.

One of the most critical steps in launching a dropshipping business is choosing a niche. In the vast world of e-commerce, finding a specific target market can help you stand out from the competition. Your niche should ideally be something you're interested in and knowledgeable about, but it also needs to have demand in the market. For example, selling general clothing might make it difficult to compete with established brands, but focusing on a niche like sustainable activewear for women or eco-friendly pet products allows you to target a more specific audience. Niche products cater to passionate customers, which can result in higher sales and more brand loyalty.

After selecting your niche, the next challenge is finding reliable suppliers. Platforms like **AliExpress**, **Oberlo**, and **Spocket** offer dropshippers access to thousands of suppliers, but not all suppliers are created equal. It's crucial to vet potential suppliers to ensure they provide high-quality products, fast shipping, and good customer service. Poor-quality products or long shipping times can lead to negative reviews, customer dissatisfaction, and ultimately, the failure of your business.

Once you've established a relationship with a supplier, it's time to build your online store. Platforms like **Shopify**, **WooCommerce**, and **BigCommerce** provide user-friendly tools for creating an e-commerce website, even if you don't have technical experience. Shopify, in particular, is a popular choice among dropshippers due to its easy integration with dropshipping apps like Oberlo, which streamlines the process of importing products from suppliers into your store and fulfilling orders.

Designing your store is a critical aspect of building trust with potential customers. A clean, professional-looking website with high-quality images, clear product descriptions, and easy navigation can make the difference between a visitor making a purchase or leaving your site. It's also important to create a seamless checkout process. Complicated or lengthy checkout processes can lead to cart abandonment, so make sure that your store is optimized for fast, user-friendly transactions.

However, simply creating a store is not enough. The real challenge lies in driving traffic to your site and converting that traffic into sales. Marketing is essential to the success of any dropshipping business. Paid advertising is one of the most effective ways to promote your store, with platforms like **Facebook** and **Instagram** offering advanced targeting options that allow you to reach your ideal customers based on demographics, interests, and behaviors. By creating visually appealing ads that showcase your products and direct users to your website, you can start generating traffic and sales.

SEO (Search Engine Optimization) is another important marketing strategy. By optimizing your website and product descriptions with relevant keywords, you can improve your store's visibility in search engine results, driving organic traffic to your site. Additionally, content marketing, such as starting a blog or creating how-to videos related to your niche, can establish your brand as an authority in your field and attract potential customers.

Influencer marketing can also be a powerful tool for dropshippers. Partnering with social media influencers who have large followings in your niche can help build credibility and drive traffic to your store. For example, if you're selling eco-friendly beauty products, partnering with a beauty influencer who promotes sustainable living can significantly increase your brand's visibility.

While dropshipping offers many advantages, it's not without its drawbacks. One of the biggest challenges dropshippers face is the lack of control over the supply chain. Since you're relying on third-party suppliers to fulfill orders, you don't have direct control over product quality, shipping times, or inventory levels. This can lead to issues like stockouts, long shipping times, or defective products. To mitigate these risks, it's essential to maintain open communication with your suppliers and regularly monitor their performance.

Customer service is another area where dropshippers can face difficulties. Since you're not physically handling the products, resolving issues like lost shipments, product defects, or returns can be more complicated. Providing excellent customer service is crucial to maintaining customer satisfaction and building a loyal customer base. Be proactive in addressing customer concerns, and work closely with your suppliers to resolve any issues as quickly as possible.

In addition to managing customer service, dropshippers must also be mindful of their profit margins. While dropshipping eliminates the need for upfront inventory costs, the profit margins are often lower compared to traditional retail models. Because you're purchasing products from suppliers at a wholesale price and marking them up for retail, your margins may be slim, especially if you're competing on price. To increase profitability, focus on offering value beyond just price—whether that's through exceptional customer service, unique product offerings, or branding that resonates with your audience.

Despite these challenges, dropshipping remains an attractive option for entrepreneurs looking to enter the e-commerce space with minimal risk. By selecting the right niche, building a professional store, and implementing effective marketing strategies, you can create a profitable dropshipping business that offers the flexibility to run from anywhere in the world.

YouTube

Building a Brand through Video

YouTube has transformed from a video-sharing platform to one of the most powerful tools for building personal brands and businesses. With over two billion monthly users, the platform offers immense potential for creators who are ready to tap into this expansive audience. Whether you're a content creator looking to share your expertise, an entertainer building a fanbase, or a business looking to increase visibility, YouTube offers unparalleled opportunities for growth.

The first step in launching a successful YouTube channel is identifying your niche. Similar to blogging or online courses, focusing on a specific topic helps you stand out in a saturated market. The most successful YouTubers are those who cater to a defined audience, whether it's a gaming channel, beauty tutorials, tech reviews, or fitness advice. Your passion for your niche will fuel your creativity, while your consistency in producing content will help you build a loyal audience. Once you find your niche, developing a content strategy is critical to success.

A key to YouTube success is creating consistent, high-quality content. Quality doesn't always mean expensive production equipment; many successful YouTubers started with a simple camera or even their smartphones. What truly matters is that your content is engaging, informative, or entertaining enough to keep your viewers coming back. Over time, you can invest in better equipment such as cameras, microphones, and lighting, but the value of your content will always be paramount. Whether you're creating vlogs, tutorials, product reviews, or how-to guides, each video should provide value to your audience.

Beyond just creating content, one of the greatest advantages of YouTube is its search functionality. YouTube is the second-largest search engine in the world, so optimizing your videos for search is crucial. This involves using the right keywords in your video titles, descriptions, and tags. By doing so, you can increase the likelihood of your videos appearing in search results when users look for content related to your niche. For example, if your channel focuses on fitness, your videos should contain specific keywords like "home workout for beginners" or "full-body exercises." The better your SEO strategy, the more visibility you'll have.

Creating eye-catching thumbnails and writing compelling video titles also play a huge role in attracting viewers. A thumbnail is the first impression your video makes, and a well-designed one can increase your click-through rate significantly. The title should be clear, concise, and designed to pique curiosity. But, be careful not to fall into the trap of "clickbait"—misleading titles might get clicks in the short term, but they'll hurt your channel's credibility and cause viewers to distrust your content over time.

Monetization on YouTube comes in several forms, and it's one of the most exciting aspects of building a channel. One of the primary methods is through the YouTube Partner Program, which allows creators to earn money from ads placed on their videos. To qualify, your channel needs to meet certain criteria, such as having at least 1,000 subscribers and 4,000 hours of watch time within the past 12 months. Once eligible, you can start earning ad revenue based on the number of views your videos receive. The more viewers and watch time you accumulate, the more ad revenue you'll generate.

However, ad revenue alone is often not enough to make YouTube a full-time income stream, which is why many creators diversify their earnings. Sponsorships are a common way for established YouTubers to make money, especially as their audience grows. Brands may approach you to promote their products or services in exchange for payment. The key to successful sponsorships is aligning with brands that are relevant to your content and that your audience will trust. For example, a tech review channel might partner with a gadget company to review their latest products, or a beauty vlogger might collaborate with a makeup brand.

Affiliate marketing is another effective way to monetize a YouTube channel. By promoting products in your videos and including affiliate links in the video description, you can earn a commission for every sale made through those links. For instance, if you're running a cooking channel, you might recommend kitchen tools or ingredients, linking to the products through affiliate programs like Amazon Associates.

Creating and selling merchandise is another option for YouTubers looking to diversify their income. Once you have built a loyal audience, you can design and sell products like t-shirts, mugs, or other branded merchandise related to your channel. YouTube even has integrations with platforms like Teespring, making it easy for creators to set up a store and sell directly to their viewers.

Engagement is a critical factor for success on YouTube. It's not enough to just upload videos; you need to build a community around your content. Responding to comments, asking viewers for feedback, and encouraging them to like, share, and subscribe helps build a loyal following. Engaging with your audience also improves your standing in YouTube's algorithm, increasing the visibility of your videos. YouTube favors content that generates likes, comments, and shares, so the more interactive your channel is, the more likely your videos are to be recommended to other users.

While YouTube offers incredible opportunities for growth, it also comes with challenges. One of the main hurdles is consistency. Building a YouTube channel takes time, and many creators struggle with maintaining a regular upload schedule. To combat this, it's important to plan your content in advance. Creating a content calendar can help you stay organized and ensure that you're consistently delivering fresh material to your audience. Setting realistic goals for how frequently you can produce videos is also important. Whether it's once a week or once a month, consistency is key.

Another challenge is dealing with negative feedback. As your channel grows, you'll inevitably encounter criticism, and not all of it will be constructive. It's important to develop a thick skin and not let negative comments derail your efforts. Focus on the positive feedback, engage with your supporters, and use any constructive criticism to improve your content.

For those who are dedicated, YouTube can be an extremely rewarding platform. It allows you to reach a global audience, build a personal brand, and generate multiple streams of income. The key to long-term success lies in creating valuable content, engaging with your audience, and being consistent in your efforts. Whether you're just starting out or looking to take your existing channel to the next level, YouTube offers endless opportunities for growth and success.

PODCASTING

Growing Your Audience through Voice

Podcasting has emerged as one of the fastest-growing mediums for content creation, allowing entrepreneurs, experts, and storytellers to share their message with a global audience. The beauty of podcasting lies in its accessibility—listeners can tune in during their commute, at the gym, or while relaxing at home, making it a convenient way to consume information. For creators, it offers an intimate way to connect with audiences, build authority in a niche, and even generate income through sponsorships, ads, and premium content.

Starting a podcast requires minimal equipment compared to other content creation mediums like YouTube. With just a quality microphone, recording software, and a platform to host your episodes, you can begin sharing your voice with the world. However, to create a successful podcast, you need more than just the right equipment. It requires thoughtful planning, consistency, and an understanding of what will resonate with your target audience.

The first step in launching a podcast is choosing your niche and format. Like other online businesses, focusing on a specific niche will help you attract a dedicated audience. Whether you're passionate about business, personal development, storytelling, or pop culture, selecting a niche that aligns with your interests and expertise is crucial for long-term success. A clearly defined niche also helps potential listeners find your podcast amidst the sea of available content.

Once you've chosen your niche, you'll need to decide on a format for your podcast. Some of the most popular formats include solo shows, where you share your thoughts or expertise; interview-style podcasts, where you bring on guests to discuss various topics; and panel discussions, which feature multiple hosts or guests in a conversational format. Storytelling podcasts, which weave together narratives like true crime, history, or fiction, have also become increasingly popular. Each format offers unique advantages, so choose one that suits your style and strengths as a creator.

Creating engaging content is essential for growing your podcast audience. Listeners tune in to podcasts for value, whether that's entertainment, education, or inspiration. The most successful podcasts keep their audience hooked by providing consistent, high-quality episodes. Planning your episodes in advance and scripting or outlining your main points will help you stay focused and deliver a cohesive message.

Audio quality is another critical factor in podcasting success. While content is king, poor audio quality can quickly turn listeners away. Investing in a good microphone and recording software will significantly improve the production value of your podcast. Fortunately, there are affordable options available for those just starting out. Programs like **Audacity** or **GarageBand** can be used for editing your audio, while more advanced software like **Adobe Audition** provides greater control for those looking to produce highly polished episodes.

Once your podcast is recorded and edited, you'll need a hosting platform to distribute your episodes. Popular podcast hosting platforms like **Buzzsprout**, **Libsyn**, and **Anchor** provide all the tools you need to upload your episodes, manage your RSS feed, and distribute your podcast to directories like **Apple Podcasts**, **Spotify**, **Google Podcasts**, and more. Choosing the right hosting platform is important, as it ensures that your episodes reach as many listeners as possible.

Marketing your podcast is one of the most challenging aspects of growing your audience. Simply uploading episodes won't be enough to attract listeners—you need to actively promote your podcast and engage with your audience. Social media is one of the most effective ways to spread the word about your podcast. Create profiles for your podcast on platforms like Instagram, Twitter, and Facebook, and regularly post updates, behind-the-scenes content, and snippets of upcoming episodes to generate excitement.

Email marketing is another powerful tool for promoting your podcast. Building an email list allows you to send new episodes directly to your subscribers, along with exclusive content or early access to special episodes. Encourage your listeners to sign up for your mailing list by offering value, such as bonus content, downloadable resources, or transcripts of episodes.

Collaborating with other podcasters is an excellent way to grow your audience. Guest appearances on other podcasts in your niche expose you to new listeners who are likely to be interested in your content. Similarly, inviting guests onto your own podcast not only adds value to your episodes but also encourages cross-promotion, as your guests will often share their appearance with their own audience.

Monetizing your podcast typically happens once you've built a loyal and engaged listener base. One of the most common monetization methods is through sponsorships. Brands pay podcasters to feature their products or services in episodes, often in the form of short ad reads at the beginning or middle of the show. To attract sponsors, it's important to have clear analytics on your listenership, including download numbers, engagement rates, and audience demographics. The more niche and targeted your audience, the more attractive your podcast becomes to potential sponsors.

Another way to monetize your podcast is through listener support. Platforms like **Patreon** allow podcasters to offer exclusive content, ad-free episodes, or bonus episodes to paying subscribers. This model works well for podcasters with dedicated audiences who are willing to pay for premium content. Some creators also offer merchandise, such as branded t-shirts, mugs, or other products, as another income stream.

Finally, podcasting allows for creative freedom. You can experiment with different formats, introduce new segments, or evolve your content based on listener feedback. However, it's essential to stay true to your niche and your audience. Consistency in your release schedule and content is key to keeping your listeners engaged and growing your subscriber base. Whether you're uploading weekly or bi-weekly, setting expectations and delivering on them will help you maintain a loyal audience.

One of the main challenges for podcasters is managing time and effort. Between recording, editing, marketing, and engaging with your audience, podcasting can become a time-intensive endeavor. It's important to pace yourself and avoid burnout. Consider outsourcing tasks like editing or show notes to free up time for content creation. Planning your episodes in advance and batching your recording sessions can also help streamline the production process.

Podcasting is more than just a business—it's a platform for building relationships with your audience. Unlike video or written content, podcasts allow for a unique connection between the creator and the listener. There's something intimate about hearing a voice in your ears, and that connection is what makes podcasting such a powerful tool for building a brand and community.

With the right niche, format, and content strategy, podcasting offers incredible opportunities for growth and income. Whether you're looking to share your expertise, tell stories, or entertain, podcasting provides a platform to reach a global audience while building a sustainable business

AFFILIATE MARKETING

Earning through Strategic Partnerships

A ffiliate marketing is one of the most popular ways to earn passive income online. It offers the potential to make money by promoting products or services from other companies and earning a commission for every sale made through your referral. The beauty of affiliate marketing is that it doesn't require you to create your own product—your role is to connect your audience with relevant products or services that align with their needs and interests.

To understand how affiliate marketing works, it's important to grasp the basic structure. When you sign up for an affiliate program, the company provides you with unique referral links or codes that track any sales made through those links. When someone clicks your link and makes a purchase, you earn a commission. The percentage you earn can vary widely, depending on the industry and the specific affiliate program you're participating in.

Affiliate marketing offers a relatively low barrier to entry. You don't need a large audience to start, but the more engaged your audience is, the more successful you'll be. If you already have a blog, YouTube channel, podcast, or social media presence, affiliate marketing can be seamlessly integrated into your existing content strategy.

The first step to success in affiliate marketing is selecting the right products or services to promote. It's essential to choose products that align with your niche and that your audience will find valuable. For example, if you run a tech blog, you could promote gadgets, software, or digital tools that you personally use and recommend. Promoting irrelevant products can erode your audience's trust and hurt your credibility, so always prioritize quality and relevance over potential commission rates.

Once you've identified relevant products, the next step is to apply for affiliate programs. Some of the most popular affiliate networks include **Amazon Associates**, **ShareASale**, **CJ Affiliate**, and **Rakuten Advertising**. These networks act as intermediaries between companies and affiliates, offering access to a wide range of products and services that you can promote. Each network has its own approval process, and some may require a certain level of traffic or engagement before you're accepted.

Creating high-quality content is key to converting your audience into buyers. Whether you're writing blog posts, creating YouTube videos, or posting on social media, your content should focus on genuinely helping your audience make informed decisions. Product reviews, how-to guides, and comparison articles are particularly effective at driving affiliate sales because they provide in-depth information that helps your audience understand the benefits of the product.

For example, a travel blogger might create a review of the best travel backpacks, including affiliate links to each product.

Transparency is vital in affiliate marketing. Always disclose when you're using affiliate links, either through a disclaimer at the beginning of your content or by explicitly stating that you earn a commission if readers make a purchase through your links. This not only ensures you comply with legal guidelines but also builds trust with your audience. Readers are more likely to support you if they understand how affiliate marketing works and know that you're being upfront about your recommendations.

SEO (Search Engine Optimization) plays a crucial role in affiliate marketing success. By optimizing your content for search engines, you can attract organic traffic to your affiliate links. Conducting keyword research to find out what your audience is searching for and incorporating those keywords into your blog posts, video titles, and descriptions can improve your visibility in search engine results. For example, if you're promoting fitness equipment, you might optimize your content for keywords like "best home workout gear" or "top-rated resistance bands."

In addition to SEO, email marketing is an effective strategy for boosting affiliate sales. Building an email list allows you to nurture relationships with your audience and share personalized product recommendations. You can create targeted campaigns that highlight specific affiliate products, offer discounts or promotions, and provide exclusive content to your subscribers. The more value you provide to your audience, the more likely they are to trust your recommendations and make purchases through your affiliate links.

One of the biggest challenges in affiliate marketing is scaling your income. Initially, your earnings may be modest, but with consistent effort, you can grow your audience and increase your conversions over time. Diversifying the products you promote and experimenting with different content formats can help you reach new audiences and maximize your earnings. For instance, if you've been primarily focusing on blog posts, consider branching out into video content or social media to expand your reach.

Tracking and analyzing your performance is also crucial for long-term success. Most affiliate programs provide detailed analytics on clicks, conversions, and earnings, which allows you to identify which products and strategies are driving the most revenue. By monitoring your data, you can refine your approach and focus on promoting the products that resonate most with your audience.

Affiliate marketing is not a get-rich-quick scheme. It takes time to build an engaged audience and establish trust with your readers or viewers. However, for those who are patient and persistent, affiliate marketing can become a significant source of passive income. The key to success is building genuine relationships with your audience, promoting products you believe in, and continuously optimizing your content and marketing strategies.

As your affiliate marketing business grows, you can explore higher-paying affiliate programs or even negotiate custom deals with brands. Some affiliates eventually move beyond simply promoting other companies' products and start creating their own digital products or services, leveraging their audience to maximize earnings.

In summary, affiliate marketing offers a powerful way to monetize your content and build a sustainable online business. By focusing on quality over quantity, providing value to your audience, and using strategic marketing techniques, you can turn your affiliate partnerships into a reliable income stream. As you continue to grow your platform, affiliate marketing can open doors to even more lucrative opportunities, allowing you to scale your business and achieve long-term success.

FREELANCE WRITING

Turning Words into Income

F reelance writing has long been a popular way to make money online, offering flexibility, creativity, and the ability to turn your writing skills into a business. Whether you're crafting articles, copywriting for businesses, ghostwriting books, or producing content for blogs, freelance writing allows you to leverage your ability to communicate through words. The demand for quality writing continues to grow, making it one of the most accessible and lucrative online ventures for those with a knack for storytelling or a strong command of language.

The first step in becoming a successful freelance writer is to identify the kind of writing that aligns with your strengths. Freelance writing encompasses a broad range of niches, including journalism, copywriting, technical writing, creative writing, and content creation. Understanding your own skill set will help you choose the right type of writing to pursue. For example, if you have a talent for persuasive writing, you might excel in copywriting for advertising or sales pages. On the other hand, if you're more comfortable with factual, research-based writing, content writing for blogs or technical writing might be a better fit.

Once you've identified your niche, the next step is building a portfolio. A strong portfolio is essential for landing freelance writing jobs, as it showcases your skills and gives potential clients a taste of your work. If you're just starting out and don't have a lot of published material, don't worry—there are several ways to build a portfolio from scratch. You can write sample articles or blog posts in your chosen niche and publish them on platforms like **Medium**, or even start your own blog to demonstrate your expertise. Guest posting on other websites or offering free content to nonprofits or small businesses can also help you build credibility.

As you begin to build your portfolio, you'll also need to market yourself to potential clients. Freelance marketplaces like **Upwork**, **Fiverr**, and **Freelancer** are great places to start. These platforms connect freelancers with businesses looking for writers and provide an easy way to start getting paid for your work. However, competition on these platforms can be stiff, so it's important to position yourself well by highlighting your unique skills and experience. Additionally, many freelancers choose to create their own website, which acts as a personal brand hub where they can showcase their portfolio, list their services, and provide contact information.

Pitching is another vital skill in freelance writing. While freelance marketplaces can be helpful, many successful writers find work through cold pitching—reaching out directly to businesses, blogs, or publications that might need content. Crafting a well-written, personalized pitch is key to standing out in a sea of generic inquiries. When pitching, always research the company or publication to understand their tone and content needs, and explain how your skills and experience align with their goals.

As a freelance writer, it's important to understand the business side of things. This includes setting rates, managing contracts, and ensuring that you're paid fairly for your work. Many new writers make the mistake of underpricing their services in an effort to attract clients, but this can lead to burnout and undervalue your skills. Research the going rates for freelance writers in your niche and set competitive, fair prices based on your experience and the scope of the project. Hourly rates are common, but many freelancers charge per word or per project, depending on the type of writing and the client's needs.

Managing time and workload is another critical aspect of freelance writing. As a freelancer, you are essentially running your own business, which means balancing multiple projects, meeting deadlines, and maintaining good relationships with clients. Setting realistic deadlines and sticking to them is crucial to building a reputation as a reliable writer. To manage time effectively, many freelancers use productivity tools like **Trello** or **Asana** to keep track of assignments and deadlines, helping them stay organized.

Freelance writing can be an incredibly rewarding career, but it also comes with challenges. One of the biggest challenges is dealing with the unpredictability of freelance work. There will be times when you have more work than you can handle, and other times when you may struggle to find clients. Diversifying your income streams by working with multiple clients and exploring different types of writing can help smooth out the ups and downs.

Another challenge is handling client feedback. Not every client will love your work right off the bat, and learning to handle constructive criticism is an essential part of freelance writing. Being open to revisions and edits while maintaining clear boundaries about the scope of work is important for building long-term relationships with clients. Setting clear expectations at the beginning of a project, including the number of revisions included in your rate, can prevent misunderstandings later.

As you gain more experience, you'll also want to focus on building long-term relationships with clients. Repeat business is the lifeblood of freelance writing. By providing high-quality work, meeting deadlines, and being easy to work with, you can turn one-off projects into ongoing partnerships. Many freelancers find that as they build relationships with clients, they can charge higher rates and rely less on constantly searching for new work.

Ultimately, freelance writing offers the freedom to work from anywhere, set your own hours, and choose the projects you want to work on. It's a career path that rewards creativity, discipline, and persistence. With dedication and the right strategy, freelance writing can become a sustainable and profitable business, allowing you to earn a living doing what you love.

GRAPHIC DESIGN

Monetizing Creativity Online

G raphic design has always been a sought-after skill, but the rise of digital platforms has transformed it into a lucrative online business. Whether you're creating logos, web graphics, social media visuals, or even print designs, the internet has made it easier than ever to connect with clients from all over the world. If you're artistically inclined and skilled in design software like Adobe Illustrator, Photoshop, or even simpler tools like Canva, you have the potential to turn your creativity into a sustainable income stream.

The first step to building a successful graphic design business online is to identify your niche. Graphic design is a broad field that includes logo design, web design, branding, product packaging, and more. Specializing in a particular area can help you stand out in a crowded market and attract clients looking for specific expertise. For instance, if you're passionate about branding, you could focus on helping small businesses develop cohesive visual identities through logos, business cards, and social media templates.

Once you've identified your niche, you'll need to start building your portfolio. A strong portfolio is essential in graphic design because clients need to see examples of your work before they hire you. Even if you're just starting out, you can create sample projects to showcase your skills. For example, you could design mock logos for imaginary businesses, create website mockups, or develop branding packages for nonprofits or friends who need design work. The key is to demonstrate your versatility and creativity, which will help potential clients understand your style and capabilities.

As you build your portfolio, you'll also need to market yourself. Graphic designers have several options for finding clients online. Freelance marketplaces like **Upwork**, **Fiverr**, and **99designs** allow you to bid on projects or showcase your work to potential clients. While these platforms can be competitive, they provide a good starting point for new designers looking to gain experience and build their reputation. Another option is to create your own website to showcase your portfolio and services. A well-designed website can act as your online business card, giving potential clients a place to view your work, learn more about your services, and contact you for projects.

Social media is another powerful tool for graphic designers. Platforms like **Instagram**, **Pinterest**, and **Behance** are visually driven, making them ideal for sharing your design work. Posting regularly, using relevant hashtags, and engaging with other designers can help you build a following and attract clients. You can also join design communities or participate in online challenges to gain exposure and connect with other creatives.

Once you start landing clients, it's important to understand the business side of graphic design. This includes setting your rates, managing client relationships, and ensuring you're compensated fairly for your work. Many new designers struggle with pricing, often undercharging in an effort to secure clients. However, it's essential to research industry rates and charge appropriately for your skill level and the complexity of the project. You may charge hourly, per project, or create packages based on the client's needs. As your experience grows, so should your rates.

Managing client relationships is another critical component of running a successful graphic design business. Clear communication is key, especially when it comes to understanding client expectations and delivering work on time. Create contracts that outline the scope of the project, payment terms, and the number of revisions included in your price. This helps avoid misunderstandings and ensures that both you and your client are on the same page from the start.

One of the challenges graphic designers face is keeping up with changing trends and technologies. Design trends evolve rapidly, and staying relevant requires continuous learning. Subscribing to design blogs, attending webinars, and practicing with new tools can help you stay ahead of the curve and keep your skills sharp. Additionally, investing in your own creative projects can keep you inspired and push the boundaries of your design capabilities.

Diversifying your income streams is another way to grow your graphic design business. In addition to offering services to clients, many designers create and sell digital products such as design templates, fonts, or graphic bundles. Platforms like **Etsy**, **Creative Market**, and **Gumroad** allow you to sell your designs to a global audience. Selling digital products is a great way to generate passive income, as you create the product once and sell it repeatedly without additional effort.

Another option for expanding your business is offering design courses or tutorials. If you're an experienced designer with a knack for teaching, you can create and sell online courses on platforms like **Udemy** or **Skillshare**, or even host your own webinars. Teaching others not only generates income but also helps you establish authority in your field, attracting more clients in the process.

Graphic design is a dynamic and creative field that offers immense opportunities for those willing to put in the work. While the competition can be fierce, the demand for high-quality design work is always strong, especially as more businesses recognize the importance of professional branding and online presence. By honing your skills, building a solid portfolio, and marketing yourself effectively, you can turn your passion for design into a profitable online business.

Virtual Assistant Services

Providing Remote Business Support

The demand for virtual assistant (VA) services has surged in recent years as businesses increasingly rely on remote support to handle administrative, creative, and operational tasks. Offering virtual assistant services is an excellent opportunity for those with strong organizational, communication, and problem-solving skills to build a flexible, scalable business. Whether you specialize in managing emails, scheduling, social media, customer service, or bookkeeping, virtual assistants are the backbone of many small businesses, entrepreneurs, and even large corporations.

Starting a virtual assistant business begins with understanding your strengths and the types of services you can offer. Some virtual assistants focus on administrative tasks, such as managing emails, scheduling meetings, and data entry, while others offer more specialized services like social media management, content creation, or customer service. Think about your skills and experiences—if you have a background in marketing, for example, you might offer services related to content marketing, email campaigns, or SEO management. If you're organized and detail-oriented, offering administrative support might be the perfect fit.

Once you've identified your core services, the next step is building your portfolio. While virtual assistants typically don't need a portfolio in the traditional sense, showcasing your skills and abilities is still crucial. A simple website outlining your services, testimonials from previous clients, or case studies demonstrating how you've helped businesses streamline their operations can go a long way in attracting potential clients. If you're just starting, you can offer discounted or even free services to a few clients in exchange for testimonials and experience.

Marketing yourself as a virtual assistant requires a strategic approach. Freelance marketplaces like **Upwork**, **Fiverr**, and **Freelancer** are excellent platforms for finding your first clients, but they are also competitive. To stand out, you'll need to create a compelling profile that highlights your skills, work ethic, and ability to meet deadlines. Social media, particularly LinkedIn, can also be a valuable tool for networking with business owners and professionals who might need your services. Joining VA groups on Facebook or LinkedIn can help you connect with fellow virtual assistants, share tips, and even find client referrals.

As a virtual assistant, building strong relationships with your clients is key to long-term success. Clear communication is critical when working remotely, as clients will rely on you to manage tasks efficiently and without constant supervision.

Setting expectations from the start—such as outlining the tasks you'll handle, your availability, and response times—will help foster trust and ensure that both you and your client are on the same page.

Managing your time is another crucial aspect of virtual assistant work. Since most VAs handle multiple clients at once, time management and organization are essential. Tools like **Trello**, **Asana**, and **ClickUp** can help you manage projects, prioritize tasks, and keep track of deadlines. Additionally, many virtual assistants use time-tracking software like **Toggl** or **Clockify** to ensure they're billing clients accurately for their work.

One of the advantages of being a virtual assistant is the ability to scale your business. As you gain more clients, you can begin to specialize in high-demand areas, such as social media management or executive assistance, allowing you to charge higher rates for specialized services. Many VAs also choose to transition into virtual assistant agencies, hiring subcontractors to handle tasks for multiple clients while focusing on business development and client acquisition.

Rates for virtual assistants can vary widely depending on the type of services offered, experience level, and client needs. While new VAs may start with lower rates to build their client base, experienced virtual assistants often charge $25 to $50 per hour, or more, for specialized services like bookkeeping, digital marketing, or project management. Offering packaged services, such as a monthly retainer for a set number of hours, can help stabilize your income and provide clients with predictable pricing.

As your virtual assistant business grows, you may want to offer additional services that can further help your clients. For example, if you're already managing a client's social media accounts, you could offer content creation or graphic design services as an add-on. If you're handling administrative tasks, you could upsell services like email marketing management or customer support. The key is to continuously adapt and evolve your offerings based on the needs of your clients.

However, like any business, virtual assistance has its challenges. One of the biggest difficulties virtual assistants face is finding clients consistently. Marketing yourself and your services requires ongoing effort, especially in the early stages when you're building your reputation. Networking, joining professional groups, and staying active on freelance platforms can help ensure you're always attracting new clients.

Another challenge is managing client expectations. Some clients may not fully understand what a virtual assistant can and cannot do, which can lead to miscommunications or unrealistic expectations. Having clear contracts, setting boundaries, and communicating effectively are essential to maintaining a healthy work-life balance and ensuring that both you and your clients are satisfied with the working relationship.

Despite these challenges, the benefits of running a virtual assistant business are numerous. You can work from anywhere, set your own hours, and choose the clients and projects that interest you most. For those who value flexibility, independence, and helping others run their businesses more efficiently, becoming a virtual assistant can be a highly rewarding career.

In conclusion, providing virtual assistant services is an excellent business opportunity for individuals with strong organizational skills and a desire to work remotely. With the right marketing strategy, clear communication, and efficient time management, you can build a thriving VA business that offers flexibility, independence, and the potential for growth. As businesses increasingly rely on remote support, the demand for virtual assistants is only expected to grow, making this a promising field for aspiring entrepreneurs.

TRANSCRIPTION SERVICES

Turning Audio into Text

The demand for transcription services is growing, driven by the surge of online content, remote meetings, podcasts, and other audio-visual materials. Transcription involves converting spoken language from audio or video files into written text, and it's a task that requires precision, attention to detail, and excellent listening skills. For anyone with a good ear and fast typing abilities, transcription offers a flexible and scalable online business opportunity.

Transcription is a versatile field, and it offers different paths depending on your interests and expertise. You can choose to focus on general transcription, which encompasses a wide range of audio material, from business meetings and interviews to podcasts and webinars. General transcriptionists work across many industries, providing accurate written records of audio files. Alternatively, medical transcription and legal transcription are two highly specialized areas that require familiarity with medical or legal terminology, and sometimes specific certification or training. These fields can be more lucrative but may require additional study.

One of the greatest advantages of starting a transcription business is the low barrier to entry. You don't need extensive education or expensive equipment to get started. The essential tools include a good computer, quality headphones, and transcription software. While many transcriptionists use basic programs like **Express Scribe** or **oTranscribe**, investing in transcription software that allows you to control playback speed and insert timestamps can make your work more efficient. Many transcriptionists also use a foot pedal, which allows for hands-free control of audio playback, significantly speeding up the transcription process.

For those who want to improve their efficiency, automated transcription software like **Otter.ai** or **Trint** can provide rough drafts of transcripts. While these programs are not 100% accurate, especially for poor-quality audio or multiple speakers, they can save time by providing an initial transcription that you can then edit. However, manual transcription remains the most accurate method, especially for content requiring high levels of precision, such as legal and medical transcripts.

To succeed in transcription, improving both your speed and accuracy is critical. Many transcriptionists are paid by the audio minute or hour, so faster transcription leads to higher earnings. However, speed must be balanced with accuracy. Clients expect error-free transcriptions, particularly in specialized fields like law or medicine where even minor mistakes can have significant consequences. Transcriptionists who take the time to proofread their work before submitting it build a reputation for reliability and quality, which can lead to repeat business and referrals.

To develop your transcription skills, practicing with a variety of audio files is essential. Audio quality varies widely, and transcriptionists often have to work with recordings that contain background noise, poor-quality sound, or multiple speakers. Becoming comfortable with these challenges will make you more efficient and effective. Over time, your listening skills will improve, and you'll develop a better ear for understanding different accents, dialects, and speech patterns.

One of the biggest challenges in transcription is dealing with difficult audio. Clients may send recordings that are unclear or feature multiple people speaking over one another, which can slow down the transcription process and lead to frustration. It's important to set expectations with clients about the quality of audio they provide and the potential impact on turnaround times. In some cases, you may need to charge extra for particularly challenging files or offer advice on how clients can improve their recordings for future projects.

Building a client base for transcription services is critical for long-term success. Platforms like **Rev, Upwork**, and **Fiverr** are excellent starting points for finding transcription work, but they can be competitive, and rates on these platforms may be lower than in private arrangements. As you gain experience, it's important to focus on direct outreach and networking to find steady clients. Creating a professional website that outlines your services, rates, and expertise can help potential clients find you more easily. Additionally, networking with professionals in industries that rely on transcription, such as healthcare, law, and media, can help you secure long-term projects.

Setting your rates as a transcriptionist depends on your expertise, the complexity of the audio, and the client's deadlines. Many transcriptionists charge by the audio minute or hour, with rates ranging from $0.50 to $3.00 per audio minute for general transcription. Specialized transcriptionists in fields like law or medicine can charge higher rates, sometimes up to $5 or more per audio minute. Some transcriptionists offer additional services, such as editing or proofreading, for an extra fee. Offering rush services for clients who need faster turnarounds can also help you earn more, though it's important to be realistic about what you can deliver within a short timeframe.

One of the challenges of transcription work is managing your time effectively. Transcription can be time-consuming, particularly for long audio files or poor-quality recordings. Many transcriptionists use time-tracking tools to monitor how long each project takes, which helps them set accurate rates and estimate how much work they can take on. It's also essential to establish clear communication with clients about deadlines and to avoid overbooking yourself. Delivering work on time is crucial for building a good reputation in the transcription industry.

Despite the challenges, transcription offers many benefits. It's a flexible, home-based business that allows you to work remotely and set your own hours. Whether you're transcribing interviews for a research project, creating written records of legal proceedings, or converting podcast episodes into text for accessibility, transcription offers a range of opportunities.

As you gain experience, you can grow your business by offering additional services, such as closed captioning or subtitling, which are in high demand in the digital age.

For those who excel in transcription, scaling your business is possible. Some transcriptionists transition from solo work to managing transcription agencies, hiring subcontractors to take on larger projects. Expanding your skillset to include editing, proofreading, or translating transcripts can also help you offer more value to your clients. As your business grows, you can focus on higher-paying clients and projects, allowing you to increase your earnings without working more hours.

In conclusion, transcription services offer a practical and profitable business model for individuals with strong listening and typing skills. By focusing on speed, accuracy, and building a steady client base, transcriptionists can create a sustainable and flexible career. With the growing demand for audio and video content across industries, transcription remains a valuable service with significant growth potential.

VOICEOVER SERVICES

Profiting from Your Voice

Voiceover services offer a unique and profitable business opportunity for those with a clear, versatile voice. From audiobooks and commercials to YouTube videos, podcasts, and animations, businesses and content creators rely on voiceover artists to bring their projects to life. The flexibility of voiceover work allows individuals to work from home, and with minimal equipment, it's possible to build a successful career in this field.

Getting started in voiceover work requires an initial investment in quality equipment. The first and most important piece of equipment is a good microphone. Popular choices among beginners include the **Audio-Technica AT2020** or **Rode NT1-A**. A pop filter helps prevent the harsh sounds of consonants from being captured, and a shock mount helps reduce vibrations during recording. To create a clean, professional sound, you'll also need a quiet, soundproof space. Many voice actors convert closets or small rooms into recording booths using acoustic foam or blankets to block out noise.

Recording software is another essential tool for voiceover artists. Programs like **Audacity** (free) or **Adobe Audition** (paid) allow you to record, edit, and enhance your audio. It's important to become familiar with these tools, as voiceover work often requires some level of audio editing, whether it's removing background noise or adjusting the volume levels to meet industry standards.

While equipment and software are important, the true skill in voiceover work comes from your ability to interpret and deliver a script. Voice acting is about much more than simply reading words—it's about conveying emotion, tone, and meaning. Whether you're recording for a corporate video, a character in an animated film, or a radio ad, understanding the client's vision and adjusting your vocal delivery to suit the project is key. Versatility is one of the most important traits of a successful voiceover artist. The more adaptable you are in your delivery, the wider range of projects you can take on.

One of the best ways to improve your voiceover skills is to practice with a variety of scripts. Many beginners start by reading books, news articles, or advertisements aloud to develop their vocal range. You can also find free practice scripts online, which cover everything from commercial reads to character dialogues. Recording yourself and reviewing the playback is essential for identifying areas where you can improve. Focus on clarity, pacing, and emotional delivery. Voice acting workshops or online courses can also provide valuable feedback and help refine your skills.

Once you feel confident in your abilities, the next step is building a demo reel. A demo reel is a short audio compilation that showcases your range as a voiceover artist. It should include different types of reads, such as commercial spots, narration, and character voices, to demonstrate your versatility. Your demo reel is essentially your portfolio, and it's what potential clients will use to determine if you're the right fit for their project. Keep it short—about one to two minutes long—and ensure the audio quality is professional.

Finding work in voiceover services can initially seem daunting, but there are multiple avenues to explore. Freelance platforms like **Upwork**, **Fiverr**, and **Voices.com** connect voice actors with clients looking for talent. These platforms are a great place to start, especially if you're looking to build your portfolio. However, they can be competitive, and rates may be lower for beginners. As you gain experience and build a reputation, you can command higher rates and find more consistent work.

Direct outreach to production companies, ad agencies, and content creators can also help you land voiceover jobs. Many businesses regularly need voiceover work for corporate videos, advertisements, and social media content. Establishing relationships with these clients can lead to repeat business and long-term contracts.

Networking with other voiceover artists and joining industry communities is also essential for growing your career. Online forums, social media groups, and industry events provide opportunities to connect with other professionals, exchange tips, and find job leads. As you build relationships within the industry, you may find that other voice actors refer clients to you when they're unavailable or need a specific voice.

Pricing your voiceover services can be tricky, especially when starting out. Rates can vary widely depending on the type of project, the length of the script, and the client's budget. For example, a short commercial read might pay between $100 and $300, while audiobooks or narration for e-learning courses can pay significantly more, often in the range of several hundred to thousands of dollars depending on the length and scope of the project. Over time, you'll develop a sense of what your services are worth, and as you gain experience, you can increase your rates.

While voiceover work can be rewarding, it also comes with challenges. One of the main obstacles is the inconsistency of freelance work. Like many creative fields, voiceover can be unpredictable, with periods of high demand followed by slower times. To combat this, many voiceover artists diversify their income streams by taking on different types of projects, from commercials and corporate work to audiobooks and video games. Building a diverse portfolio of clients helps stabilize your income and opens you up to a wider range of opportunities.

In conclusion, voiceover services offer a creative and flexible business opportunity for individuals with a talent for vocal delivery. By investing in quality equipment, honing your voice acting skills, and marketing yourself effectively, you can build a successful career in this growing field. With persistence and practice, voiceover work can become a profitable and enjoyable way to use your voice to earn a living.

COACHING AND CONSULTING

Guiding Others to Success

C oaching and consulting have become popular ways for individuals with expertise in specific areas to share their knowledge, help others grow, and build a business. Whether you're a life coach, business consultant, or specialized in areas like fitness, finance, or career development, the coaching and consulting industry is thriving. As more people seek personal development and businesses look for experts to solve specific problems, the demand for coaches and consultants has steadily increased.

One of the main attractions of this field is the ability to work closely with clients, offering personalized advice and guidance tailored to their unique needs. Coaching involves helping individuals set goals, overcome obstacles, and achieve success in areas such as personal growth, relationships, or career. Consulting, on the other hand, typically focuses on providing professional or technical advice to businesses or organizations in areas like marketing, operations, leadership, and strategy.

The first step to starting a coaching or consulting business is to identify your area of expertise. Successful coaches and consultants usually specialize in a particular niche, whether it's business growth, wellness, career transitions, or leadership development. Your niche should reflect both your skills and your passion. If you have a background in fitness and a passion for helping people transform their lives, fitness coaching might be a perfect fit. If you have experience managing teams or driving business growth, consulting for small businesses or startups could be highly rewarding.

Once you've chosen your niche, it's essential to establish credibility. Clients want to work with someone who is knowledgeable and experienced. This doesn't always mean you need formal certification—though in certain fields, like life coaching, certifications from accredited institutions can help build trust. Often, real-world experience, proven results, and testimonials from satisfied clients can be just as effective. Establishing your online presence through a website, blog, or social media accounts is another way to showcase your expertise and attract clients.

Building a coaching or consulting business often starts with offering one-on-one services. Many new coaches begin by working directly with clients, either through in-person meetings or virtual sessions via platforms like Zoom or Skype. This personalized approach allows you to deeply understand your clients' needs and deliver tailored advice that helps them achieve their goals. As your business grows, you can expand into group coaching, workshops, webinars, or even create digital products like e-books or online courses that complement your services.

Setting your rates as a coach or consultant depends on your niche, experience level, and the value you provide to clients. Some coaches charge hourly rates, while others offer packages that include a certain number of sessions. Consultants often charge by the project or offer retainer agreements for ongoing support. High-level executive coaching or consulting for large corporations can command premium rates, while personal coaching for individuals might start at lower price points. Regardless of your pricing model, it's important to clearly communicate the value you bring to the table and how your services can help clients achieve their goals.

Marketing is essential for growing your coaching or consulting business. Networking is a powerful tool for connecting with potential clients. Attending industry events, joining professional associations, and even hosting your own webinars or workshops can help you build a reputation and establish yourself as an expert in your field. Additionally, content marketing—such as writing blog posts, creating YouTube videos, or sharing insights on social media—can attract potential clients by showcasing your knowledge and providing valuable advice for free.

Another key aspect of success in coaching or consulting is building strong relationships with your clients. People seek coaches and consultants because they want personalized attention and guidance. Being an active listener, showing empathy, and demonstrating genuine care for your clients' success is essential for fostering long-term relationships. Many successful coaches and consultants rely heavily on referrals, so maintaining high levels of client satisfaction is crucial.

As your business grows, you may want to explore opportunities to scale. One way to do this is by transitioning from one-on-one coaching to group programs or workshops. Group coaching allows you to work with multiple clients simultaneously, increasing your impact and income potential without requiring more hours in the day. You can also create online courses, write a book, or offer digital products that allow you to reach a wider audience and provide additional revenue streams.

However, coaching and consulting also come with challenges. One of the biggest hurdles is managing client expectations. Some clients may expect immediate results or may not fully understand the work required on their part to achieve their goals. Setting clear expectations from the outset—both in terms of what you will deliver and what they need to do— can help prevent misunderstandings. It's also important to establish boundaries with clients, particularly when working remotely. Clear communication about availability, response times, and the scope of work is essential for maintaining a healthy work-life balance.

Another challenge is the emotional labor involved in coaching. Helping others navigate personal or professional challenges can be incredibly rewarding, but it can also be emotionally draining. Coaches and consultants need to practice self-care and set personal boundaries to avoid burnout.

In conclusion, coaching and consulting offer a fulfilling and profitable business opportunity for those with expertise in a particular field. By guiding others to success—whether it's in their personal lives, careers, or businesses—you can make a real impact while building a scalable and sustainable business. With the right marketing strategy, client relationships, and continuous professional development, coaching and consulting can become a long-term, rewarding career path.

Web Development and Design

Creating Digital Experiences

W eb development and design are at the heart of the digital world, with businesses and individuals relying on websites to create an online presence, market their products, and engage with audiences. As a web developer or designer, your role is to build these digital experiences, combining technical expertise with creative flair. It's an industry with immense demand, offering flexibility, scalability, and high earning potential.

To begin a career in web development, you need a strong foundation in programming languages like HTML, CSS, and JavaScript, which form the backbone of website functionality. For those focused on design, proficiency in graphic design software like Adobe XD or Figma, alongside an understanding of user experience (UX) principles, is crucial for creating intuitive, aesthetically pleasing websites. Combining these two skill sets is invaluable, as full-stack developers who can handle both the front-end (what users see) and back-end (what powers the site behind the scenes) are highly sought after.

Many developers start their journey by learning to build small websites for friends, local businesses, or personal projects. These initial experiences help you build a portfolio that showcases your skills. A strong portfolio is essential because potential clients will want to see examples of your work before hiring you. As your portfolio grows, you can start approaching larger clients or even niche industries, such as e-commerce or nonprofits, where specialized web solutions are needed.

In terms of career paths, web developers and designers have several options. You can work as a freelancer, allowing you to control your schedule and projects. Alternatively, you can build a web design agency, where you manage a team of designers and developers, taking on larger projects. Another option is to work in-house for a company, creating and maintaining their digital properties. The advantage of freelancing or running an agency is that it offers flexibility and the ability to scale your business as demand grows.

Pricing your services is one of the more complex parts of web development and design. Some developers charge by the hour, with rates ranging from $50 to $150 or more, depending on experience and project complexity. Others charge per project, with rates varying widely based on the scope of work. Simple websites may cost a few thousand dollars, while more complex sites with e-commerce functionality, custom features, or extensive back-end systems can run into the tens of thousands. Offering additional services, such as website maintenance, hosting, or SEO (Search Engine Optimization), can also increase your income while providing clients with a comprehensive package.

One of the key challenges in web development is keeping up with the rapid pace of technological change. The tools, frameworks, and languages used in web development evolve quickly, and developers need to stay updated with the latest trends and best practices. Continuous learning is crucial. Subscribing to industry blogs, taking online courses, or participating in coding communities will help you stay ahead. For example, new frameworks like React or Vue.js have gained popularity for building dynamic web applications, and understanding how to use them will make you more competitive in the market.

Working with clients can also present challenges, particularly when managing expectations or dealing with revisions. Communication is key. Setting clear goals and deadlines, discussing the scope of work upfront, and ensuring that both parties understand what's achievable within the timeline and budget can help prevent misunderstandings. Web development projects often require ongoing communication, with developers and clients working closely together to ensure the final product meets expectations.

As your web development business grows, you may find opportunities to scale by hiring other developers, designers, or project managers. Running a web development agency allows you to take on larger projects and manage a team, but it also introduces new responsibilities, such as business development, team management, and client relations. Balancing these roles effectively can help you grow your agency while maintaining the quality of work that initially attracted clients.

Ultimately, web development and design offer endless opportunities. It's a field where creativity meets technology, allowing you to build something tangible that has a real impact on clients and their businesses. With the right skills, a strong portfolio, and effective client management, you can build a successful and sustainable career in this growing industry.

STOCK PHOTOGRAPHY

Selling Your Images

S tock photography is an excellent business opportunity for photographers looking to monetize their work by licensing images to companies, websites, and creatives worldwide. Stock images are used in marketing materials, blogs, social media, and print publications, offering a steady stream of demand for quality photos. For photographers, this model allows you to earn passive income—once your photos are uploaded to stock sites, they can be licensed repeatedly, generating revenue long after the shoot.

To succeed in stock photography, photographers need to understand the market demand. Stock agencies are looking for images that serve commercial purposes—such as lifestyle, travel, business, technology, and nature shots. While artistic photos may be beautiful, stock images are typically purchased by businesses looking for photos that fit specific purposes. Therefore, focusing on universally relevant topics, such as people working in offices, families enjoying outdoor activities, or food photography, will increase the chances of your photos being licensed.

Many photographers start their stock photography business by contributing to well-established platforms like **Shutterstock**, **iStock**, or **Adobe Stock**. These platforms offer global exposure, allowing your photos to reach a wide audience. The submission process typically involves uploading your images and providing descriptive titles, tags, and keywords to help buyers find your photos. Understanding SEO for stock photography—by using relevant, descriptive keywords—will increase the visibility of your images on these platforms.

It's important to note that stock photography is a volume game. The more high-quality photos you upload, the higher your chances of generating sales. Many successful stock photographers have portfolios with hundreds or even thousands of images across different categories. Consistently producing and uploading new content ensures a steady flow of potential income.

Photographers should also focus on technical quality. Stock agencies have strict guidelines for photo submissions, and images need to be well-composed, correctly exposed, and free of imperfections like noise or lens flare. Investing in good equipment, such as a DSLR camera and sharp lenses, is crucial for producing images that meet stock photography standards. Editing software like **Adobe Lightroom** or **Photoshop** can help fine-tune images before submission, ensuring they're polished and professional.

Another important consideration is obtaining model releases for any recognizable people in your images. Stock agencies require model releases to protect themselves and the photographers from legal issues. Without proper releases, images with identifiable faces cannot be sold. Similarly, location releases may be needed for photos taken on private property or in restricted locations.

While the initial income from stock photography may seem modest, earnings can grow significantly over time, especially if you build a diverse portfolio and regularly upload new images. Some photographers also diversify by contributing to multiple stock platforms or by offering exclusive photos, which can command higher prices.

Marketing your stock portfolio through social media or a personal website can also help drive traffic to your photos and increase your sales. Sharing your images on Instagram, Pinterest, or photography blogs, with links to purchase them through stock agencies, gives you additional visibility and builds your brand as a photographer.

The challenge of stock photography is competition. With millions of images available on stock platforms, standing out requires a combination of creative composition, technical excellence, and a deep understanding of what buyers are looking for. Staying current with trends in the stock photography market—such as the increasing demand for diversity and inclusion in images—can help you create photos that are both relevant and sellable.

In conclusion, stock photography offers photographers an opportunity to turn their passion into passive income. By understanding the market, producing high-quality images, and consistently uploading new content, photographers can build a portfolio that generates ongoing revenue. While the competition is stiff, the demand for fresh, relevant images remains strong, making stock photography a viable business model for those with the right skills and perseverance.

PRINT ON DEMAND

Selling Custom Merchandise without Inventory

Print on demand (POD) has emerged as a convenient and low-risk way to start an online business, particularly for creative entrepreneurs who want to sell custom merchandise. It allows you to create unique designs and sell products like t-shirts, mugs, hoodies, posters, and tote bags without ever needing to hold inventory or manage shipping. POD platforms such as **Printful**, **Teespring**, **Redbubble**, and **Zazzle** handle the production and fulfillment processes for you. When a customer places an order, the product is printed and shipped directly from the POD provider.

One of the main advantages of POD is the low upfront cost. Traditional e-commerce businesses often require large investments in inventory and storage, but with POD, you only pay for the product once it's sold. This makes it a particularly attractive option for individuals who want to test different designs or niches without risking significant capital. Additionally, POD allows for complete creative freedom—whether you're an artist, graphic designer, or simply someone with clever ideas, you can upload designs, set your pricing, and market your products.

To succeed in the POD space, it's essential to focus on **finding a niche**. Generic designs may struggle to stand out in a crowded market, but niche products that cater to a specific audience can attract a loyal customer base. For example, designing products around eco-friendly messages, specific hobbies like hiking or gaming, or even memes and pop culture references can help you capture the attention of a focused group of buyers.

Creating designs that resonate with your niche is key to building a successful POD business. You don't need to be a professional graphic designer to get started; tools like **Canva** or **Procreate** make it easy to create visually appealing designs, even if you're a beginner. If design isn't your strong suit, you can also collaborate with freelance designers on platforms like **Upwork** or **Fiverr** to bring your ideas to life.

Once you have your designs ready, you'll need to build an online storefront. Many POD platforms integrate with e-commerce solutions like **Shopify**, **Etsy**, or **WooCommerce**, allowing you to set up a professional-looking store with relative ease. Having your own store gives you more control over branding, customer experience, and pricing, although selling directly on POD marketplaces like Redbubble can still be an excellent way to reach new audiences without the need to drive traffic to your own website.

Marketing is a crucial component of any successful POD business. Social media platforms like **Instagram**, **Pinterest**, and **TikTok** are great places to showcase your designs and engage with potential customers. These platforms are particularly effective for visually-driven products, and creating consistent, high-quality content can help you build an audience. Additionally, paid advertising—whether through **Facebook Ads**, **Google Ads**, or **Pinterest Ads**—can give your products more exposure and drive traffic to your store. Another effective strategy is using influencer marketing. Partnering with influencers who align with your niche can help boost your brand and encourage their followers to check out your products.

Pricing your products effectively is another important step. You'll need to account for the base cost of the product, the fees charged by the POD provider, and your desired profit margin. Researching similar products in your niche can give you a good idea of what customers are willing to pay, but it's important not to undervalue your work. Offering discounts or limited-time promotions can also encourage first-time buyers and help build brand loyalty.

While POD offers many advantages, it's not without its challenges. One of the main difficulties is the **profit margin**, which can be relatively slim depending on the POD platform's base costs. This means you need to focus on driving volume or offering higher-end products with larger margins. Additionally, because POD companies handle the production and shipping, you have little control over fulfillment times or product quality. It's crucial to work with reliable POD providers and test the products yourself to ensure they meet your quality standards.

Another challenge is standing out in a competitive marketplace. With so many creators and sellers entering the POD space, building a unique brand and engaging with your target audience is more important than ever. Developing a clear brand identity, offering exceptional customer service, and constantly refreshing your designs can help you stay ahead of the competition.

In summary, print on demand offers an exciting opportunity for creative entrepreneurs to start an online business with minimal upfront costs. By focusing on finding a niche, creating compelling designs, and marketing your products effectively, you can build a successful POD business that grows over time. With persistence and creativity, POD can become a steady source of income, and as your business scales, you can explore additional ways to diversify your product line and grow your brand.

App Development

Creating and Monetizing Digital Solutions

In today's technology-driven world, app development has become one of the most lucrative and exciting business opportunities. Whether it's creating mobile applications, web-based tools, or software as a service (SaaS), the possibilities are endless for developers who can identify problems and create digital solutions to solve them. App development doesn't just appeal to large corporations; even small startups and solo entrepreneurs can build successful apps with the right idea and strategy.

The first step in creating a successful app is **identifying a problem or need**. Apps that solve real problems or provide users with meaningful convenience are the ones that stand out in the marketplace. This could be anything from simplifying everyday tasks to creating entirely new ways for people to interact with technology. For example, Uber revolutionized the transportation industry by solving the problem of getting a reliable ride quickly, while fitness apps like **MyFitnessPal** provide users with a way to track their health and fitness goals.

Once you have identified a problem your app can solve, the next step is **planning and designing**. At this stage, you'll need to define your app's features, functionality, and overall user experience (UX). Apps that are easy to use, intuitive, and aesthetically pleasing tend to be more successful. Sketch out the user interface (UI), decide how users will interact with the app, and think about what features are most important. Prioritize simplicity in design and make sure that the core features are seamless before adding more complex functionality.

Many app developers start by building **MVPs (Minimum Viable Products)**. An MVP is the simplest version of your app that still provides value to users. It allows you to test your concept in the real world with minimal development costs, gather feedback from early users, and make adjustments before launching a more polished version. For those with limited coding skills, app development tools like **Flutter**, **React Native**, or **OutSystems** allow you to build MVPs without deep programming knowledge.

When it comes to developing the app itself, you'll need to decide whether to build it for **iOS**, **Android**, or both. While iOS apps typically reach a more affluent audience, Android has a larger user base globally. Cross-platform development tools like **React Native** or **Xamarin** allow you to create apps that work on both platforms, saving time and effort.

Monetizing your app is one of the most critical steps in turning your idea into a business. There are several ways to monetize an app, depending on your business model. Some apps use a **freemium model**, where basic features are free, but users must pay for premium features or content. **In-app**

purchases and **advertising** are also common revenue models, especially for mobile games and social apps. If your app solves a significant problem for businesses, offering it as a **subscription-based service** (SaaS) could provide a steady revenue stream.

Once your app is built, you'll need to **market** it effectively. Launching an app doesn't guarantee success—millions of apps are already available in app stores, so standing out requires a solid marketing strategy. Begin by building a pre-launch buzz through social media, email marketing, and influencer partnerships. Setting up a landing page for your app can also help capture early interest and allow you to build an email list of potential users. Paid advertising, particularly on platforms like **Facebook**, **Instagram**, and **Google Ads**, can also help drive traffic to your app.

Another critical component of app success is **gathering user feedback**. Launching your app is only the beginning. You'll need to continuously improve it based on user reviews and behavior. Analytics tools like **Firebase** or **Google Analytics** for apps can provide valuable insights into how users are interacting with your app, which features are most popular, and where users are dropping off. This feedback loop allows you to iterate on your app, fix bugs, and add new features that keep users engaged.

App development is not without its challenges. One of the biggest obstacles is the **cost of development**. Hiring developers, designing the UI/UX, testing the app, and maintaining it over time can be expensive. For solo entrepreneurs, this can be a significant barrier to entry. Many turn to investors, crowdfunding platforms, or business loans to cover the costs of development. Additionally, finding the right developers and project managers is critical to ensuring that the app is built on time, on budget, and according to your vision.

Another challenge is the **competition**. With millions of apps in the marketplace, getting noticed can be tough. Focusing on solving a specific problem or targeting a niche audience can help your app stand out. Instead of trying to build an app that appeals to everyone, hone in on a particular user base with unmet needs. For example, rather than building a general fitness app, you could create an app specifically for new mothers looking to regain fitness after pregnancy.

As your app grows, so do your opportunities for scaling the business. Many successful apps eventually expand their offerings, either by adding new features, launching complementary apps, or exploring new markets. A strong focus on **user retention**—keeping users engaged and coming back to the app—is key to ensuring long-term success. Features like push notifications, in-app messages, or gamification elements (such as rewards or achievements) can enhance user engagement and improve retention rates.

User acquisition is just the beginning. Retention and maintaining a loyal user base are vital for generating recurring revenue. Offering continuous updates, addressing bugs promptly, and integrating user feedback helps keep your app fresh and relevant. Engaging with your community through social media, customer support, and even hosting user forums can help users feel connected to your brand and app.

Another pathway to scaling your app is exploring **partnerships** and collaborations. For instance, partnering with other apps, businesses, or influencers in your niche can open doors to new user bases. If your app integrates well with other platforms, such as fitness tracking apps syncing with smart devices, it can increase its usability and appeal.

If your app becomes highly successful, you might consider **monetizing through acquisition**. Many developers eventually sell their apps to larger companies looking to expand their portfolios. Whether through acquisition or mergers, selling an app can lead to a substantial payday, especially if the app has a solid user base and proven revenue model.

Challenges in scaling include managing growing operational costs (such as servers and data storage), customer support, and keeping the app secure from hackers or data breaches. Addressing these challenges effectively is essential as a growing user base requires more resources to maintain performance and security.

In conclusion, app development offers vast opportunities for entrepreneurs with the technical skills and vision to solve problems through digital solutions. The path to success involves careful planning, iterative development, and smart marketing strategies to build a loyal user base. Whether you're building a simple utility app or an innovative SaaS solution, the possibilities are endless if you focus on solving user needs and continuously improving your product.

SEO CONSULTING

Helping Businesses Grow Online

In the digital age, a strong online presence is essential for businesses, and **Search Engine Optimization (SEO)** is the key to being found online. SEO consultants specialize in improving a website's visibility on search engines like Google, which directly impacts traffic, leads, and sales. For anyone with a passion for digital marketing and an analytical mindset, SEO consulting can be a highly lucrative business.

The role of an SEO consultant is to **analyze a client's website** and identify opportunities to optimize it for search engines. This involves conducting **keyword research** to understand what potential customers are searching for and implementing strategies that make the website more attractive to search engines. These strategies might include optimizing title tags, meta descriptions, internal linking structures, and content to align with target keywords.

SEO consulting also involves **on-page** and **off-page SEO** tactics. On-page SEO focuses on the technical elements of the website, such as load times, mobile responsiveness, and clean code, while off-page SEO involves strategies like

backlink building (getting other websites to link to your client's site). Both elements are critical for improving a site's ranking on search engine results pages (SERPs).

One of the first steps for SEO consultants is conducting an **SEO audit** of the client's website. This audit uncovers technical issues that may be hindering the site's performance in search results, such as broken links, slow loading times, or missing alt text. By fixing these problems, SEO consultants can improve a site's usability and search engine visibility.

Once the technical elements are optimized, **content strategy** becomes a priority. Search engines favor websites that regularly publish high-quality, relevant content, so part of your role as an SEO consultant will be advising clients on the types of blog posts, landing pages, and multimedia content they should produce. Often, content is built around the keywords identified during research, helping businesses attract organic traffic.

SEO consulting is highly data-driven. You'll use tools like **Google Analytics**, **Ahrefs**, **SEMrush**, and **Moz** to track website performance, analyze traffic sources, and measure the effectiveness of your SEO strategies. These tools provide insights into which keywords are driving traffic, how long users are staying on the site, and where there are opportunities for improvement.

A challenge in SEO consulting is managing **client expectations**. SEO is a long-term investment, and it can take months to see significant results. It's important to communicate this to clients from the outset to avoid frustration. Setting clear goals, such as improved keyword rankings, increased traffic, or enhanced site authority, helps clients understand what to expect and when.

SEO consultants can charge by the hour, offer monthly retainers, or work on a project basis. Rates typically range from $75 to $200 per hour, depending on experience and the complexity of the project. Offering **ongoing SEO services**, such as monthly audits and continuous optimization, can create long-term relationships with clients and provide steady income.

In conclusion, SEO consulting is a critical service in today's digital landscape, helping businesses increase their online visibility and reach their target audience. For consultants who enjoy problem-solving and working with data, this field offers both financial rewards and the satisfaction of helping businesses grow.

SaaS (Software as a Service)

Creating Subscription-Based Tools

S oftware as a Service (SaaS) is a business model where software is provided as a service, rather than as a one-time product, usually via subscription. SaaS platforms like **Dropbox**, **Slack**, and **Salesforce** have revolutionized industries by offering users access to powerful tools without needing to download, maintain, or update software themselves. For entrepreneurs with a technical background or a strong vision for solving a specific problem, SaaS offers incredible opportunities.

The core of a SaaS business is developing **cloud-based software** that solves a particular problem or makes a process more efficient. SaaS solutions are widely used in industries like project management, marketing, customer relationship management (CRM), and accounting, but new niches are emerging every day. The challenge and opportunity in SaaS lie in identifying an underserved market and building a product that offers real value to businesses or individuals.

Building a SaaS platform typically requires a combination of programming, **user experience design**, and a clear understanding of the target market's pain points. Many successful SaaS companies start by developing a **Minimum Viable Product (MVP)** to test their concept with early adopters. The MVP is a stripped-down version of the software that includes only the most essential features. This allows entrepreneurs to gather feedback, iterate on the product, and refine it before investing in a full-scale launch.

The subscription model is one of the most appealing aspects of SaaS businesses. By offering software through a **monthly or annual subscription**, you create recurring revenue streams that provide more stability compared to one-time product sales. SaaS businesses often use **tiered pricing models**, where users can choose between different subscription levels, each offering additional features or benefits. This allows for flexibility in pricing and attracts a wide range of customers.

Another important aspect of SaaS is **scalability**. Once the initial product is developed, the cost of onboarding new users is relatively low, which means that SaaS businesses can grow rapidly with the right marketing and product improvements. The goal is to build a product that can serve hundreds or thousands of customers with minimal ongoing costs. This scalability makes SaaS one of the most attractive business models in the tech industry.

However, building and maintaining a SaaS product comes with its challenges. **Customer retention** is critical—since users are paying on a subscription basis, it's essential to keep them engaged and satisfied with the product. Regular updates, new features, and excellent customer support are all necessary to reduce churn and keep users from canceling their subscriptions.

Another challenge is **security**. Because SaaS platforms handle large amounts of user data, maintaining robust security protocols is essential to protect sensitive information and comply with regulations like GDPR. Any data breaches or security failures can lead to loss of trust, legal consequences, and significant damage to your business's reputation.

In conclusion, SaaS offers a powerful business model with recurring revenue and the potential for significant growth. By identifying a market need, developing a scalable product, and focusing on customer satisfaction, entrepreneurs can build highly successful SaaS businesses that serve users across industries.

Domain Flipping
Trading Digital Real Estate

D omain flipping, much like real estate investing, involves buying domain names and selling them at a profit. With millions of websites being launched each year, a premium domain name can be a valuable asset. Entrepreneurs who master the art of domain flipping can make significant profits by buying domain names that are in demand, undervalued, or have potential future value, then selling them to interested buyers.

The first step in domain flipping is identifying valuable domain names. Short, memorable names that include common words or industry-specific keywords tend to have the most value. For example, domains like health.com or finance.com are worth millions, but even niche domains like bestworkoutgear.com or organicfoodsupply.com can command high prices if they cater to a specific market with high demand.

Domains related to trending topics or emerging industries can also be lucrative. For instance, when cryptocurrency became popular, domain names with "crypto" or "blockchain" in them became highly valuable. Anticipating future trends or changes in the market can help domain flippers identify opportunities before they become mainstream.

Buying and selling domain names, known as domain flipping, can be an incredibly profitable business if done strategically. Once you've registered valuable domains, the next step is to market and sell them for a profit. Websites like **Flippa**, **Sedo**, and **GoDaddy Auctions** are popular platforms where domain buyers and sellers interact. To maximize profits, it's essential to understand which domains are in demand and how to present your domains as premium assets.

When pricing your domain, consider factors such as length (shorter domains are typically more valuable), keyword relevance, brandability, and the current market trends. For example, a domain with a single common word or phrase can command a much higher price than a domain with random or uncommon combinations of words.

Negotiating with buyers is another important aspect of domain flipping. Some buyers will make an initial offer, while others might need some persuasion to see the value in your domain. Being patient and having a good sense of the market can help you close more lucrative deals. Offering installment plans or leveraging domain brokerage services can also help facilitate the sale.

Another strategy is **domain parking**, which allows you to earn revenue from a domain while waiting for a buyer. Domain parking services display advertisements on your domain's landing page, and you earn money when visitors click on those ads. While this won't generate significant revenue unless your domain has substantial traffic, it's a way to monetize your asset until it sells.

The risks in domain flipping include purchasing domains that don't increase in value or paying too much upfront for domains that may not sell for a profit. Research is key—using tools like **Namebio** (which tracks domain sales) or studying the domain market to understand what types of domains are selling will help mitigate these risks. It's also essential to avoid buying trademarked names, as this can lead to legal complications.

In conclusion, domain flipping offers a low-barrier, high-potential business model for those willing to research, invest strategically, and market their assets. With careful domain selection, negotiation, and patience, domain flipping can become a profitable venture in the digital real estate market.

SELF-PUBLISHING

Becoming an Author in the Digital Age

Self-publishing has revolutionized the way authors bring their work to market, allowing writers to bypass traditional publishing houses and take control of the entire process—from writing to production to marketing. Platforms like **Amazon Kindle Direct Publishing (KDP)**, **Smashwords**, and **IngramSpark** have democratized the publishing process, making it easier for aspiring authors to publish and sell their books worldwide.

The first step in self-publishing is to write a manuscript that will resonate with your target audience. Whether you're writing fiction, non-fiction, or even poetry, it's essential to focus on quality, as the competition in self-publishing is fierce. Editing is critical, and many self-published authors hire professional editors to ensure their book is polished and free of errors. In addition to editing, having a professional cover design is key to attracting readers—first impressions matter, especially in a crowded marketplace like Amazon.

Once your manuscript is complete, you'll need to format it for publication. Platforms like Amazon KDP offer built-in tools to help you format your book for both e-books and print versions. It's important to ensure your book looks professional, with proper spacing, fonts, and layout. The ease of distribution through platforms like Amazon means your book can reach readers across the globe, but success still relies heavily on your ability to market and promote your book.

Marketing your self-published book requires strategic planning. While having your book available on Amazon or another platform is important, simply uploading it and waiting for sales won't work. Successful self-published authors use a variety of marketing tactics, such as building an author website, engaging with readers through social media, and running paid ads on platforms like **Facebook** or **Amazon Ads**. Many authors also build email lists by offering free chapters or exclusive content to potential readers in exchange for their contact information. This allows authors to build a relationship with their audience and promote future books directly.

Another powerful marketing tool is **book reviews**. Getting reviews on platforms like Amazon or Goodreads can significantly impact your book's visibility and sales. Many self-published authors offer advance copies of their book to readers or book bloggers in exchange for honest reviews. Positive reviews build credibility and can help persuade new readers to buy your book.

One of the greatest advantages of self-publishing is the control it gives authors over their work. You retain all rights to your book and receive a larger percentage of royalties compared to traditional publishing. Amazon KDP, for instance, offers royalties of up to 70%, while traditional publishers typically offer much lower percentages. However, this control also means you're responsible for everything—from writing and editing to cover design and marketing—which can be both empowering and overwhelming.

In addition to publishing on platforms like Amazon, some self-published authors expand their reach by selling directly through their websites or offering special editions of their books. This allows you to create more personalized experiences for your readers and potentially earn higher profits by avoiding platform fees.

While self-publishing offers significant opportunities, it's also a highly competitive field. One of the biggest challenges self-published authors face is standing out in the marketplace. Consistency is key—many successful self-published authors release multiple books per year, building a backlist that attracts more readers over time. The more titles you have available, the more likely readers are to discover your work.

In conclusion, self-publishing offers an accessible path for writers to bring their work to market and earn an income. By focusing on producing high-quality content, leveraging marketing tools, and building a strong relationship with readers, self-published authors can find success and thrive in the digital age.

MEMBERSHIP SITES

Building Exclusive Communities and Recurring Income

Membership sites offer a fantastic business model for content creators, educators, or professionals who want to build exclusive communities while generating recurring income. By offering premium content, services, or access to a private community, membership sites allow you to monetize your knowledge or expertise on a subscription basis.

The first step in creating a membership site is choosing a **niche** and determining the type of content or services you'll offer. Successful membership sites typically provide ongoing value to their members, whether through educational resources, exclusive video content, workshops, or access to a private forum. Examples of popular membership sites include fitness coaches offering workout plans and meal guides, business mentors providing live Q&A sessions, or artists sharing behind-the-scenes content and tutorials.

Once you've determined your niche, you'll need to choose a platform to host your membership site. Platforms like

Patreon, **Kajabi**, **Teachable**, and **MemberPress** make it easy to create and manage membership sites. These platforms offer tools for uploading content, managing subscriptions, and interacting with your community. The choice of platform depends on your specific needs—some platforms are more suited for video-based content, while others excel at community-building or educational resources.

Pricing your membership tiers is an important consideration. Many membership sites use a **tiered pricing model**, where subscribers pay different amounts for access to various levels of content or perks. For example, a basic tier might provide access to exclusive blog posts or videos, while higher tiers offer personalized coaching, live webinars, or downloadable resources. Offering multiple pricing options allows you to cater to different audience segments and increase your revenue potential.

Marketing your membership site involves building awareness and attracting a loyal community. Social media, email marketing, and content marketing are essential tools for promoting your site. Many successful membership site owners create **lead magnets**, such as free content or webinars, to attract potential members. Offering a free trial or discounted introductory membership can also help you convert visitors into paying members.

Retaining members is just as important as acquiring them. The value of a membership site lies in its ability to generate **recurring income**, so keeping members engaged and satisfied is crucial. Regularly adding new content, offering personalized interactions, and fostering a sense of community can help reduce churn and keep members subscribed for the long term.

Membership sites also offer opportunities for scaling. As your community grows, you can expand your offerings or even bring in guest experts to provide additional value. Some membership site owners diversify their income streams by offering one-off products, live events, or premium workshops to their members, creating multiple revenue streams within the same platform.

In conclusion, membership sites offer a scalable and sustainable business model for entrepreneurs and creators who want to share their expertise and build a dedicated community. By consistently delivering value, engaging with your members, and focusing on retention, you can build a thriving membership business with recurring income and long-term success.

FITNESS COACHING

Taking Training to the Digital World

The fitness industry has embraced the digital world, with online fitness coaching offering trainers the ability to reach a global audience and expand their client base beyond in-person sessions. Whether you specialize in personal training, nutrition coaching, or yoga, transitioning your fitness coaching business online can provide flexibility, scalability, and the potential for greater income.

Starting an online fitness coaching business requires building a strong **personal brand**. Clients seek coaches who they trust and connect with on a personal level, so developing a recognizable brand that reflects your style, values, and expertise is essential. Whether your niche is weight loss, strength training, or holistic wellness, focusing on a specific area allows you to stand out in a crowded market.

Offering customized training plans is one of the key components of online fitness coaching. Many coaches use fitness apps or platforms like **Trainerize**, **TrueCoach**, or **My PT Hub** to deliver personalized workouts, track progress, and communicate with clients. These platforms allow you to monitor your clients' progress, provide feedback, and adjust their training plans as needed, ensuring that each client gets the attention they need.

Nutrition coaching is another popular service that can be offered alongside training plans. Many clients look for holistic approaches to fitness that combine exercise and diet, and online fitness coaches can create meal plans, track caloric intake, and provide personalized nutrition advice through platforms like **MyFitnessPal** or **Eat This Much**. Combining both fitness and nutrition coaching can lead to better results for your clients, helping them achieve their goals faster and making your coaching program more comprehensive.

Delivering high-quality content, whether through personalized training plans, video tutorials, or educational materials on nutrition and wellness, is key to standing out as an online fitness coach. Content creation also plays a major role in marketing your business. Platforms like **Instagram**, **YouTube**, and **TikTok** are excellent for sharing fitness tips, workout snippets, or client success stories, helping to build a following and attract new clients. Hosting live sessions, offering free challenges, or collaborating with other fitness influencers can also help expand your reach and credibility in the industry.

Building a fitness coaching business online offers flexibility in terms of location and time. You can work with clients from around the world, tailoring your services to their needs and offering packages that fit their schedule and budget. Group training sessions, one-on-one coaching, or even online fitness courses allow you to create various revenue streams. Some coaches also offer subscription services, where clients get access to ongoing support, workout plans, and exclusive content in exchange for a monthly fee.

One challenge online fitness coaches often face is maintaining accountability and motivation for their clients without in-person sessions. This is where regular communication becomes key—whether through check-ins, progress reports, or video calls, staying connected with your clients will help keep them engaged and motivated. Additionally, offering community support through private groups or forums where clients can interact with each other can foster a sense of accountability and encourage progress.

In conclusion, fitness coaching in the digital world opens up new opportunities for reaching clients and expanding your business beyond the confines of a gym. By building a strong personal brand, leveraging digital tools, and offering valuable, comprehensive coaching services, you can create a thriving online fitness business. With a focus on both training and nutrition, online fitness coaching can provide personalized solutions that help clients achieve their health and wellness goals.

SOCIAL MEDIA MARKETING

Helping Brands Grow Digitally

S ocial media has become an indispensable tool for businesses looking to grow their brand, connect with audiences, and drive sales. Social media marketing involves creating and executing strategies to promote a brand's products or services through platforms like **Instagram**, **Facebook**, **Twitter**, **LinkedIn**, **TikTok**, and more. As a social media marketer, your role is to help businesses build an online presence, engage with their followers, and convert that engagement into sales.

The first step to becoming a successful social media marketer is understanding the different platforms and the type of content that works best on each. For example, Instagram is highly visual and focuses on high-quality images, stories, and reels, while LinkedIn is more business-oriented and is perfect for B2B marketing and thought leadership content. Knowing how to tailor your messaging and content to each platform is crucial.

A successful social media strategy involves both **organic content** and **paid advertising**. Organic content is the regular posting of images, videos, stories, and updates that help grow a brand's presence without paying for promotion. Paid advertising, on the other hand, involves creating targeted ads that appear in users' feeds, driving traffic to the brand's website or store. As a social media marketer, you will need to master both types of strategies to help your clients maximize their reach and engagement.

Another important element of social media marketing is **analytics**. Platforms like Instagram, Facebook, and TikTok offer built-in analytics tools that allow marketers to track engagement, impressions, clicks, and conversions. These insights are invaluable for understanding what content resonates with the audience and adjusting strategies to improve performance over time. Tools like **Hootsuite**, **Buffer**, and **Sprout Social** are also useful for scheduling posts, monitoring engagement, and analyzing metrics across multiple platforms.

Content creation is at the heart of social media marketing. Marketers are responsible for creating or curating engaging posts, videos, stories, and more that align with the brand's voice and resonate with its audience. It's essential to stay on top of trends, experiment with new types of content, and continually test what works best for a particular audience. Whether it's creating a viral TikTok video, launching an Instagram contest, or sharing behind-the-scenes content on Facebook, social media marketing requires creativity, consistency, and strategy.

In addition to organic and paid strategies, **influencer marketing** has become a key part of many social media marketing plans. Collaborating with influencers—individuals who have large, engaged followings—allows brands to reach new audiences through trusted voices. Influencers often promote products or services through sponsored posts, stories, or reviews, and their recommendations can significantly impact brand visibility and sales.

One challenge social media marketers face is staying updated with constantly changing algorithms and features on each platform. Algorithms determine which content appears in users' feeds, and changes to these algorithms can drastically impact reach and engagement. Being adaptable and continuously learning new trends and techniques is essential for success.

As a social media marketer, building strong relationships with clients is key. Understanding their brand values, audience, and goals will help you develop tailored strategies that deliver results. Whether you're working with small businesses, startups, or larger corporations, your ability to effectively communicate and execute your social media strategies will be the foundation of your success.

In conclusion, social media marketing is a dynamic and rewarding field that offers immense opportunities for helping businesses grow in the digital world. By mastering content creation, analytics, paid advertising, and influencer partnerships, you can build a successful business as a social media marketer. With billions of users across social platforms, the potential for growth and success is limitless.

DIGITAL PRODUCTS

Creating and Selling Online Assets

I n today's digital-first world, selling digital products is a lucrative business model that doesn't require physical inventory or shipping logistics. Digital products, such as e-books, online courses, templates, stock photos, music, and software, are easy to create, distribute, and sell globally. Once created, digital products can generate passive income, as they can be sold repeatedly without the need for restocking or production.

The first step in selling digital products is identifying a **niche** where your expertise can meet a demand. For instance, if you're a designer, you might create graphic templates or fonts for other designers or businesses. If you're a writer, self-publishing e-books or creating digital guides on topics you're knowledgeable about can offer a steady income stream. Entrepreneurs in the tech industry might develop software or apps, while musicians can sell tracks, sound effects, or beats.

Creating high-quality digital products requires both **technical skills** and an understanding of your target audience. Platforms like **Teachable**, **Udemy**, and **Gumroad** allow creators to easily develop and sell their digital products, providing tools to handle sales, content distribution, and customer management. Digital products can also be sold on marketplaces like **Etsy** (for digital art and templates) or **Creative Market** (for design assets).

One of the most attractive aspects of selling digital products is the **scalability**. Once you've created a product, there are no limits to how many times it can be sold. This makes it a perfect business model for individuals looking to generate passive income. However, success in this field requires an effective **marketing strategy** to ensure that your digital product reaches the right audience. Social media, email marketing, SEO, and paid advertising can all play a role in driving traffic to your product pages.

A significant advantage of digital products is that they allow creators to establish themselves as **experts in their field**. Selling e-books or online courses positions you as a knowledgeable resource, building credibility and potentially opening doors to other business opportunities such as speaking engagements, consulting, or coaching.

However, challenges include **piracy** and **competition**. Since digital products are easy to replicate, ensuring your work isn't illegally distributed can be difficult. Offering personalized support, updates, or exclusive access can help combat piracy and provide more value to paying customers. Additionally, competition can be fierce in many digital product markets, so continuous innovation and providing unique, high-quality products are essential for success.

In conclusion, selling digital products offers a flexible, scalable, and profitable business model for creators in various fields. With minimal overhead costs and the potential for passive income, digital products represent a powerful opportunity for entrepreneurs to monetize their skills and knowledge.

E-Book Publishing

Profiting from Digital Books

E-book publishing has exploded in popularity, giving authors the ability to bypass traditional publishers and sell their work directly to readers worldwide. Platforms like **Amazon Kindle Direct Publishing (KDP)**, **Apple Books**, and **Kobo Writing Life** have made it easier than ever for writers to publish and distribute their books globally. E-books are cost-effective to produce and can generate a steady stream of income for both fiction and non-fiction authors.

The first step in publishing an e-book is writing a **high-quality manuscript** that appeals to your target audience. Whether you're writing novels, self-help books, or guides, understanding your readers' preferences and delivering value is key to success. Once your manuscript is complete, you'll need to invest in **editing and formatting** to ensure that your e-book looks professional. Hiring a professional editor and using tools like **Scrivener** or **Vellum** for formatting can help ensure your book is polished and ready for publication.

Designing an eye-catching **cover** is another critical aspect of e-book publishing. While the old adage advises not to judge a book by its cover, in the digital world, the cover is often the first thing potential readers see. A professional cover design can significantly impact your book's sales. If you're not skilled in graphic design, it's worth investing in hiring a professional cover designer. Many successful self-published authors have found that an attractive cover leads to increased visibility and higher conversion rates.

Once your manuscript is complete, and your cover is designed, the next step is **publishing** your e-book. Platforms like **Amazon Kindle Direct Publishing (KDP)**, **Apple Books**, and **Kobo Writing Life** allow authors to upload their e-books, choose pricing options, and make their work available to a global audience. The process is relatively straightforward, and many platforms offer detailed guides to help authors navigate the publishing process.

Pricing your e-book is a critical decision. While traditional publishers often price e-books between $10 and $15, self-published authors typically have more flexibility. Many new authors opt for lower prices (such as $2.99 or $4.99) to attract a wider audience and generate more downloads. Pricing can also play a role in **promotional strategies**, where temporary discounts or free promotions can help boost visibility and sales, particularly in competitive genres like romance or mystery.

One of the key advantages of self-publishing is the **royalty structure**. With Amazon KDP, for example, authors can earn up to 70% royalties on their e-books, a much higher percentage than traditional publishing. This means that even if you sell your e-book at a lower price point, you can still generate significant income, especially if you build a large readership.

Marketing is essential to the success of your e-book. Simply publishing your book won't guarantee sales—effective marketing strategies are needed to build visibility. Social media platforms like **Instagram, Twitter**, and **Facebook** can help authors promote their work, while book-related platforms like **Goodreads** are valuable for connecting with readers and garnering reviews. Many authors also use **Amazon Ads** or **BookBub** to promote their e-books, targeting specific reader demographics based on genre and reading preferences.

Building an **email list** is another powerful marketing tool for self-published authors. By offering readers incentives like a free chapter or bonus content in exchange for their email address, you can create a direct line of communication with your audience. This allows you to announce new releases, share exclusive updates, and cultivate loyal readers who are eager to purchase future books.

Book reviews are crucial for building credibility and driving sales. Encouraging readers to leave reviews on platforms like Amazon or Goodreads can boost your book's visibility, as books with more reviews tend to rank higher in search results and recommendations. Positive reviews act as social proof, making your book more appealing to potential readers.

Another way to maximize the profitability of your e-book is by **expanding into other formats**. Once you've successfully published your e-book, you can explore producing **paperback** or **audiobook** versions to reach different segments of readers. Platforms like **IngramSpark** allow self-published authors to produce and distribute physical copies of their books, while services like **Audible** enable authors to create and sell audiobooks.

In addition to individual book sales, self-published authors can build a steady income by writing multiple books and creating a **backlist**. Authors with a series of books or several titles across different genres can attract more readers, as fans who enjoy one book are likely to purchase others from the same author. The more books you have available, the greater your earning potential.

While self-publishing offers immense opportunities, it also comes with challenges. One of the biggest hurdles is **competition**. With thousands of new e-books published every day, standing out in the marketplace can be difficult. To overcome this, it's important to focus on **quality writing**, **professional presentation**, and effective **marketing strategies**. Authors who consistently deliver well-written, engaging books while actively promoting their work are more likely to succeed in the crowded self-publishing space.

In conclusion, e-book publishing offers a viable and profitable path for authors who are willing to take control of the publishing process. With the right combination of quality writing, professional presentation, and smart marketing, self-published authors can generate significant income and build a dedicated readership. The flexibility, higher royalty rates, and global reach provided by platforms like Amazon KDP make e-book publishing an exciting and accessible option for writers in the digital age.

PODCASTING

Sharing Stories and Building an Audience

Podcasting has rapidly become one of the most popular ways to consume content, offering an intimate and engaging medium for sharing stories, interviews, education, and entertainment. As a podcast host, you have the opportunity to build a loyal audience, establish authority in your niche, and even monetize your show through sponsorships, ads, and listener support.

Starting a podcast requires relatively simple equipment. A **high-quality microphone** and audio editing software are essential for producing clear, professional-sounding episodes. Popular microphones for podcasters include the **Blue Yeti** and **Audio-Technica AT2020**, while software like **Audacity** (free) or **Adobe Audition** (paid) allows you to edit your audio files, clean up background noise, and enhance sound quality.

Before launching your podcast, it's important to **identify your niche** and define your target audience. Podcasts that focus on a specific theme or topic tend to attract more dedicated listeners than broad, general-interest shows. Whether you're passionate about storytelling, entrepreneurship, fitness, or comedy, finding your niche allows you to tailor your content to a particular group of listeners who are likely to engage with your episodes and become loyal fans.

Creating a **content plan** is essential for keeping your podcast organized and ensuring consistency. Many successful podcasts release episodes on a regular schedule—whether it's weekly, biweekly, or monthly. Consistency helps build a loyal audience, as listeners will know when to expect new episodes. Planning topics or interviews in advance allows you to stay on top of production and ensures that your episodes flow naturally from one to the next.

Guest interviews can add variety and depth to your podcast, and inviting experts or influencers from your industry can help attract new listeners. When booking guests, it's important to prepare thoughtful questions and provide a clear outline of the episode so your guest knows what to expect. A good interview should feel natural and conversational while offering valuable insights to your audience.

Once your podcast is recorded and edited, you'll need to **distribute** it through podcast platforms like **Apple Podcasts**, **Spotify**, **Google Podcasts**, and **Stitcher**. These platforms make it easy for listeners to discover and subscribe to your show. Hosting services like **Libsyn**, **Buzzsprout**, and **Anchor** can handle the technical aspects of uploading and distributing your episodes across multiple platforms.

Marketing your podcast is crucial for growing your audience. Social media is a powerful tool for promoting new episodes, engaging with listeners, and building a community around your podcast. Creating shareable content, such as audiograms or highlight clips, can help attract attention and drive traffic to your episodes. Collaborating with other podcasters through guest appearances or cross-promotion is another effective way to reach new audiences.

Monetizing your podcast is possible once you've built a dedicated listener base. Many podcasters earn revenue through **sponsorships** or **ads**, with companies paying to have their products or services promoted during episodes. Platforms like **Patreon** also allow listeners to support their favorite podcasts directly through monthly subscriptions in exchange for exclusive content, behind-the-scenes access, or bonus episodes.

In conclusion, podcasting is a dynamic and accessible medium for sharing your voice, building an audience, and even generating income. With the right combination of quality content, consistent production, and effective marketing, your podcast can become a valuable platform for personal expression or business growth. Whether you're looking to entertain, educate, or inspire, podcasting offers endless possibilities for creativity and connection.

EMAIL MARKETING

Building and Engaging Your Audience

Email marketing is a powerful tool for businesses and entrepreneurs to connect with their audience, nurture relationships, and drive conversions. It offers a direct and personal way to communicate with your audience, allowing you to send targeted messages based on interests, behavior, and purchase history. With a well-executed email marketing strategy, businesses can build loyalty, boost sales, and keep their audience engaged.

To start with email marketing, the first step is **building an email list**. Collecting email addresses from customers, followers, or website visitors is crucial. Offering incentives such as discounts, exclusive content, or free downloads in exchange for an email subscription can help you grow your list. Ensure that you're adhering to privacy laws, such as **GDPR**, by getting explicit consent from users to send them marketing emails.

Creating **engaging email content** is key to keeping your subscribers interested and driving conversions. Your emails should provide value, whether it's through helpful information, product updates, or exclusive offers. Segmenting your email list allows you to send more personalized content to different groups of subscribers. For example, you might send one type of email to new subscribers, another to loyal customers, and a separate email to those who haven't made a purchase in a while.

The design of your emails is also important. Using email marketing platforms like **Mailchimp**, **ConvertKit**, or **Klaviyo**, you can create visually appealing and mobile-friendly emails. Keep your design clean and simple, with a clear call to action (CTA) that directs your subscribers to take the next step, whether it's making a purchase, reading a blog post, or attending a webinar.

Automated email sequences are a highly effective way to stay engaged with your audience without needing to manually send every message. For instance, you can set up a welcome email series that automatically sends when someone subscribes to your list. Other automation options include abandoned cart reminders for e-commerce businesses or re-engagement emails for subscribers who haven't interacted with your content recently.

Measuring the success of your email campaigns is crucial for optimizing your strategy. Most email marketing platforms provide detailed analytics on open rates, click-through rates, and conversions. These metrics can help you understand what's working and where there's room for improvement. For example, if your open rates are low, you may need to improve your subject lines to be more engaging. If your click-through rates are lagging, reconsider the placement or clarity of your CTAs.

A/B testing is another powerful tool in email marketing. This involves sending two versions of an email to different segments of your list to see which one performs better. You can test various elements such as subject lines, email design, or CTAs to determine what resonates most with your audience.

One challenge email marketers face is **avoiding the spam folder**. To increase the chances of your emails being delivered and opened, make sure you're following best practices. Avoid spammy language like "FREE" in subject lines, and always provide an easy way for subscribers to opt out of your emails. Maintaining a clean email list by regularly removing inactive subscribers can also improve your deliverability rates.

In conclusion, email marketing offers a direct and effective way to engage with your audience, build relationships, and drive business growth. By focusing on list-building, creating valuable content, and leveraging automation, you can create email campaigns that yield strong results and long-term customer loyalty.

FREELANCE SERVICES

Turning Skills into Income

The gig economy has opened up countless opportunities for individuals to turn their skills into income through freelance services. Whether you're a writer, graphic designer, web developer, or marketer, freelancing allows you to work independently, set your own rates, and choose the projects that interest you most.

To start a freelance career, the first step is **identifying your skill set** and the type of services you'll offer. Some freelancers specialize in a specific niche, like technical writing or social media marketing, while others provide broader services. Creating a portfolio that showcases your work is essential for attracting clients. If you don't have much experience, consider doing a few projects for free or at a reduced rate to build your portfolio.

Freelance marketplaces like **Upwork**, **Fiverr**, and **Freelancer** make it easy to find clients, but they are competitive. To stand out, you'll need to create a compelling profile, highlighting your skills, experience, and testimonials from previous clients. Many freelancers also build personal websites to showcase their portfolio, list services, and share client testimonials, offering potential clients a direct way to hire them.

Networking plays a significant role in building a freelance business. Joining industry groups on LinkedIn or participating in forums where potential clients gather can help you find opportunities. Many freelancers rely on referrals, so building strong relationships with clients and delivering high-quality work is key to long-term success.

One of the biggest challenges freelancers face is **pricing their services**. It can be tempting to underprice your work to attract clients, but it's important to charge rates that reflect your skills, experience, and the value you provide. Some freelancers charge by the hour, while others prefer project-based fees. As you gain more experience and build a reputation, you can gradually increase your rates.

Managing multiple projects, deadlines, and client relationships can be challenging for freelancers. Tools like **Trello**, **Asana**, or **ClickUp** can help you stay organized, manage your workload, and keep track of deadlines. Time-tracking software like **Toggl** is also useful for ensuring that you're billing clients accurately.

Another important aspect of freelancing is **negotiating contracts**. Before starting any project, it's essential to have a clear agreement in place that outlines the scope of work, deadlines, payment terms, and any revisions that might be needed. Having a solid contract protects both you and the client and ensures that there are no misunderstandings about the expectations of the project.

Client retention is another key to building a successful freelance career. Repeat business is more cost-effective than constantly seeking new clients. By providing excellent service, meeting deadlines, and going above and beyond in your work, you can build long-term relationships with clients who will come back to you for future projects. Offering additional services or upselling existing clients is another way to increase your income.

In conclusion, freelancing offers freedom and flexibility for individuals looking to leverage their skills and work independently. With the right marketing strategies, client relationships, and project management, freelancers can build a thriving business that offers both financial stability and personal fulfillment.

The Journey to Building an Online Business

As we conclude this book, it's clear that the opportunities for building an online business are more abundant than ever. From selling digital products and freelance services to launching podcasts or starting a coaching business, the internet offers countless paths to success for creative and entrepreneurial minds. The beauty of online business is that it allows you to pursue your passion, work from anywhere, and build something meaningful while generating income.

However, success doesn't come without challenges. Each business model discussed in this book requires dedication, persistence, and a willingness to adapt. Whether you're creating content, offering a service, or developing a product, building an online business means embracing the ups and downs of entrepreneurship. The journey can be long, but with the right mindset and strategies, it can lead to financial independence and personal satisfaction.

The key to thriving in the digital space is to **continuously learn, experiment, and refine**. As technology evolves, so too must your business. Whether it's adapting to new social media trends, optimizing your SEO strategy, or finding innovative ways to engage with your audience, staying ahead of the curve is critical. Embrace failure as part of the process, knowing that every setback is a learning opportunity that brings you closer to success.

Equally important is **knowing your audience**. Understanding your customers' needs, preferences, and pain points allows you to offer value in ways that stand out from the competition. Focus on building trust, delivering quality, and engaging with your audience consistently. In the end, your ability to solve problems for your customers or entertain and educate them is what will set your business apart.

Finally, **take action**. Ideas are the foundation of any business, but execution is what brings them to life. Start small, test your ideas, and gradually scale. There's no perfect moment to begin, so the best time to start is now. Whether you're offering freelance services, selling e-books, or launching a membership site, take that first step with confidence and commitment.

In the digital world, there's room for everyone to succeed. As you embark on your entrepreneurial journey, remember that the most important thing is to stay focused, keep learning, and never give up. Every successful online business started with someone who believed in their vision, and with the right approach, that can be you.

The possibilities are endless—so go out there and build the business of your dreams.

GLOSSARY

(Alphabetical Order)

Affiliate Marketing: A marketing arrangement where businesses reward affiliates for driving sales through their marketing efforts, typically through referral links.

Call to Action (CTA): A prompt in marketing materials that encourages users to take a specific action, such as "Sign Up Now" or "Learn More."

Content Marketing: A strategy focused on creating valuable content to attract and engage an audience, driving profitable customer actions.

Cross-Platform Development: The process of creating software applications that can run on multiple platforms, such as iOS and Android, using tools like React Native or Flutter.

Domain Flipping: The practice of buying and selling domain names for a profit, often by finding undervalued or in-demand names.

Freelancing: Offering services on a project or contract basis, often in fields like writing, design, or marketing.

Freemium Model: A business model where basic services are offered for free, but premium features are available for purchase.

Landing Page: A standalone web page designed specifically for marketing purposes, often used in paid advertising to capture leads or drive conversions.

Lead Magnet: A free resource, like an e-book or checklist, offered to users in exchange for their contact information, commonly used in email marketing.

Membership Site: A website offering exclusive content or services to paying members, often in the form of tutorials, premium content, or specialized communities.

MVP (Minimum Viable Product): The most basic version of a product, developed to test a business idea in the market with minimal resources.

Niche: A specialized segment of the market with specific needs and characteristics, often targeted to create tailored products or services.

Pay-per-Click (PPC): An online advertising model where advertisers pay each time their ad is clicked, commonly used in platforms like Google Ads.

Print on Demand (POD): A fulfillment method where products (such as t-shirts, books, or mugs) are only produced after an order is placed, reducing the need for inventory.

SaaS (Software as a Service): A software delivery model where applications are hosted online and provided to users on a subscription basis.

Self-Publishing: The process of publishing books, usually e-books, directly to platforms like Amazon without going through traditional publishing houses.

SEO (Search Engine Optimization): The practice of improving a website's visibility in search engine results through keyword optimization, content strategies, and technical improvements.

Stock Photography: A collection of professional images licensed for use in creative or commercial projects.

Upsell: The practice of offering customers an additional or upgraded product or service after an initial purchase.

Voiceover: The process of recording a voice to be used in media such as videos, commercials, or audiobooks.

Copyrights and Credits

This book and its contents, including all chapters, text, and graphics, are the intellectual property of the author. Unauthorized reproduction, distribution, or commercial use of any part of this book is prohibited without express permission from the author.

Credits go to various online platforms, resources, and tools mentioned throughout the book, which play crucial roles in supporting online businesses. For more information, please refer to the official documentation and terms of service for tools like Amazon KDP, Shopify, Upwork, and others mentioned in the chapters.

Printed in Great Britain
by Amazon